بسم الله الرحمن الرحيم

الانصاف فى بيان سبب الاختلاف

Al-Insaf
Fi Bayan Sabab Al-Ikhtilaf

A rational explanation of

Difference of opinion in *Fiqh*

By

SHAH WALI ALLAH AL-DIHLAWI
1114-1176 AH/ 1702-1762

TRANSLATED

By
DR. MUHAMMAD ABDUL WAHHAB

Ta-Ha Publishers Ltd.
1 Wynne Road
London SW9 0BB
website : http/www.taha.co.uk

Copy© **DR. MUHAMMAD ABDUL WAHHAB**

Published July 2003
by
Ta-Ha Publishers Ltd.
1 Wynne Road
London SW9 0BB
Website: http://www.taha.co.uk
Email: sales@taha.co.uk

All right eserved. No part of this publication may be reproduced, stored in any retrieval, or transmitted in any form or by any means, electronic or otherwise, without written permission of the publishers.

Translated
by
Dr. Muhammad Abdul Wahhab

A catalogue record for this book is available from British Library.

ISBN: 1 842000 28 4

Typeset by:
Nu-Era Graphics

Printed and bound by:
De-luxe Printers, London NW10 7NR
Email: de-luxe@talk21.com

Contents

Preface

Introduction

1	Introduction by the author	9
2	A rational explanation of difference of opinion (in *Fiqh*)	21
3	The reasons for difference of opinion amongst the Companions and Followers over the *furū'*	22
4	The reasons for difference of opinion *(madhhab)* among the *Fuqaha'*	33
5	The reasons for differences between Ashab al-Hadith and Ashab al-Ra'i	43
6	*Fiqh* between the two extremes	57
7	Conditions of *Fiqh* before the 4th century- Reasons for differences between the predecessors and successors over affiliation and non-affiliation to a *madhhab*	63
8	The attitude of people towards *Fiqh* after the 4th century	81
7	Bibliography	91
8	Glossary	93
9	Index of Qur'anic verses	99
10	Index of *Ahadith*	100
11	Index of books mentioned in Arabic text	103
12	Footnotes	105

DEDICATION

In memory of my late parents who inspired me to learn Arabic and Islamic studies, but could not live long enough to enjoy the fruit of their aspirations.

PREFACE

This translation of *Al-Insaf* is a humble endeavour to introduce the noble works of Shah Wali Allah Al-Dihlawi to the English-speaking world. It is a modest tribute to his scientific investigation of the historical factors and other circumstances, which led to the development of Islamic Jurisprudence and the subsequent emergence of its different schools of thought. *Al-Insaf*'s significance to Islamic Jurisprudence does not deserve recognition merely because it is written by a scholar of repute like Shah Wali Allah. Rather, its author's fair analysis coupled with reasoned judgement, objective criticism and examination of differences among different *madhahib* also need to be seen in the wider context of his overall scheme of reforming the *Ummah* by tracing its original roots.

Al-Insaf captured my imagination when I was preparing a lecture on Shah Wali Allah for the Arabic and Islamic Cultural Society of London, in April 1993. Although I had read about Shah Wali Allah, during the course of this preparation my interest in his personality and works grew deeper and deeper. As I read through *Al-Insaf* I realised that because of its contribution and significance to Islamic Jurisprudence and *Hadith* literature, its translation into English would be a humble service to the aims of this illustrious work.

Some passages and sentences in Arabic text are very long and therefore, they have been broken into small sentences to be more clear and understandable. Such sentences are easily noticeable by the additions shown in brackets in the beginning, middle and sometimes at the end of such sentences. Most of the authors and other persons' names in Arabic text appear only with their surnames or titles and therefore their full names including their dates of deaths are added to them in brackets. There was also need for books to be mentioned with full titles which are shown in brackets.

It is hoped that this work will not only expound some of the views of Shah Wali Allah on Islamic Jurisprudence but it will also increase our awareness and understanding about the origin and development of Islamic Jurisprudence and some of its schools of thought. With the rapidly growing awareness and influence of Islam in the West, the demand for original and authentic Islamic literature has also grown, especially among the Muslims. If this translation of *Al-Insaf* contributes in any way to that end, it will fully serve the purpose of its publication.

MUHAMMAD ABDUL WAHHAB
LONDON
RAMADAN 1418
DECEMBER 1997

INTRODUCTION BY THE TRANSLATOR
1114-1176 AH /1702-1762 -AD

Shah Wali Allah al-Dihlawi does not need any introduction. He was a well-known reformer (*mujaddid*), mystic, revolutionary thinker, theologian, tradionist (*muhaddith*), jurist, sociologist, a prolific writer, poet and probably the first translator of Qur'an in Persian[1]. Much has been written and discussed about his life, works and thoughts. It is not the purpose of this work to add anything new to what has already been written by learned scholars. However, for those who are reading for the first time, or those who have not read enough about Shah Wali Allah, here it would not be out of place to shed some light on some aspects of the life, views and works of this great Muslim thinker and reformer.

Qutb al-Din Ahmad Abu'l-Fayyad Shah Wali Allah al-Dihlawi was born in Delhi about four years before the death of Mughul emperor Aurangzaib Alamgir (1027-1118AH/1618-1707AD). He descended from a noble, intellectual, spiritual and religious background. His family tree is traced back to the Second Muslim Caliph Umar ibn al-Khattab and to Shaikh Shams al-Din Mufti as the first family ancestor in India.

Shah Wali Allah's grandfather Shaikh Wajih al-Din is although referred to as *sahib al-saif wa'l-qalam* (a man of sword and pen), he was renowned for his bravery and adventurous skills. His father, 'Abd al-Rahim al-'Umari (d.1131AH/1719AD) was a great scholar and *Sufi shaikh* of his time. He is held in high esteem by the Muslim scholars of India for his contribution to the promotion of the science of *Hadith* in the Indian sub-continent. He founded a *madrasa* known after him as *Rahimiyya*, which produced many Muslim scholars. He is venerated for his piety, dignity and moderation. Although he enjoyed good standing among the religious and literary circles, it is said he avoided contact with officials and rulers. Only on the insistence of his mother he joined a committee of *'ulama'* set up to review *Al-Fatawa al-'Alamgiriyya*, a compendium of *Fiqh* according to the Hanafi school of thought. This was compiled under the direction of the Mughul emperor Aurangzaib Alamgir.

According to his biographers Shah Wali Allah was an exceptionally gifted child. He is said to have memorised the whole Qur'an at the age of seven. By the age of fifteen he completed his religious education under his father and started teaching at his *madrasa*. After the death of his father he became its Principal.

In 1143AH/1730AD Shah Wali Allah went for *hajj* and stayed there for fourteen months. During his stay in Madina he studied *Hadith* under eminent scholars of *Hadith* like Shaikh Wafd Allah b. Sulaiman al-Maghribi, Abu Tahir al-Madani, 'Abd Allah b. Salim al-Basri and Taj al-Din al-Qal'i.

Here it is worth noting that during his stay at Makkah and Madina we find no report of his contact with Muhammad b.'Abd al-Wahhab (1115-1206AH/1702-1791AD), who is generally referred to as founder of the Wahhabi movement. Neither is there any reference in Shah Wali Allah's writings about this movement. It could be that Muhammad b. 'Abd al-Wahhab was still a student and had not yet launched his movement, because until then although his views were somehow not unknown, he is known to have launched his movement after the death of his father in 1153AH/ 1740AD.

However, after his return from Hijaz, Shah Wali Allah resumed his teaching career and began writing as well. As Principal of the *madrasah* he became fully involved in its affairs. As a result of his efforts it attracted many students from various parts of the country and became a recognised centre of Islamic learning. Its educational achievements and academic progress also impressed the then Mughul emperor Muhammad Shah Rangeela, who as a gesture of recognition of Shah Wali Allah's work gave him a big building in the centre of the city.

We are told that Shah Wali Allah was a very successful teacher who applied his special methods of teaching. His teaching method was based on three stages. Firstly he would thoroughly teach his students the text of the course books. Then he would teach them the meanings of their contents, and finally teach them extensively all the minute details.[2] It would appear that this method was designed to help the students in the first place to understand the text so that they can easily grasp its meanings and deduce ideas and other objectives of the author.

Like his father, Shah Wali Allah also took special interest in the science of *Hadith*. He is believed to be the first Indian scholar who established a proper *Dār al-Hadith* (Centre for the study of *Hadith*) where he taught *Hadith* according to his own methods. He used to discuss different issues with his students in order to encourage them to utilise their creative and constructive thinking. He was also keen on bringing harmony and understanding between the followers of Hanafi and Shafi'i schools of thought in order to break the centuries old stagnation caused by narrow-mindedness and mere *taqlid*.[3]

As noticed above, there were already signs of maturity and seriousness in young Shah Wali Allah, however, after his return from Hijaz his closest family members noticed an unusual change in his attitude. His book *Fuyūd al-Haramayn*, in which he has recorded his spiritual observations and dreams he went through during this journey, portrays his image as serious thinker and visionary.

It would appear that this attitude might have been further strengthened by his broadened understanding of the conditions of Muslims, of which he probably became more aware during his contacts with scholars from various parts of the Muslim world. The weak Ottoman Empire was facing many challenges, especially regional rebellions and independent movements. Alongside this was the growing influence of Christian missionaries, and infiltration of secret agents from different European countries.

India was not an exception. As pointed out above, Shah Wali Allah was born during the reign of Aurangzaib Alamgir, who is although credited with many successes, achievements, personal piety, wisdom and political acumen, his reign also witnessed periods of turbulence and political upheavals.

What happened during Aurangzaib's ascension to the throne was repeated during the conflict between his three sons, among whom he had divided the rule of the country before his death. As a result of these civil wars the grip of the central government over the affairs of the country became weak and the tendency for rebellion and independence in provinces grew strong. The chaotic and anarchic movements of Maharattas and the Jat Rajputs further weakened this political instability. Obviously this situation attracted foreign interventions, especially the Afghan attacks because the sovereignty of the Mughul Empire was dependent on provincial rulers. The strength of provincial rulers was weakened by the Maharattas who in turn were beaten by the Afghans. It was during this period of political instability that the East India Company was trying to extend its influence in different parts of India. What happened thereafter is historically too well known to be repeated here.

Shah Wali Allah himself has very comprehensively depicted the picture of political, social, economic and cultural conditions of the society of his time. He writes: "After deep consideration I have concluded that there are two factors responsible for the corruption of culture in our time; firstly, many people have abandoned other professions and have attached themselves to the government. As a consequence the burden of their livelihood is being borne by the *Bayt al-māl* (public treasury). Some of them are professional soldiers; others are a class of scholars who feel the government should care for their livelihood. They also include court poets and lonely *dervish*, who could best be described as beggars. It has always been the tradition of kings and rulers to reward such people with presents and donations. And such people in some form or other receive some thing from *Bayt al-māl*. In short all these people whose only objective is to fill their bellies, notwithstanding the fact that whether they serve any interest or need of the society or government, they cause unfair burden on *Bayt al-māl*. And it will be in the interest of the nation and country to get rid of these people as soon as possible.

The second fault in the present culture is that the government has imposed heavy taxes on landlords, farmers, industrialists and businessmen. Add to (that misery is the pain) that for collection of these taxes these people are subjected to force. As a result loyal and obedient citizens are being suppressed under the burden of these taxes and their conditions are deteriorating, which is ruining the country. On the other hand, in contrast to these loyal and obedient citizens, there are groups of people who as a result of their discomfort with unfair taxes and suppression by officials have become rebellious, because they feel they can easily get away with their disobedience and confront the government. The best way for (the success) of the system is to impose light taxes on citizens and to fully protect their rights. The people of our time should take this point into consideration."[4]

So this was the society in which Shah Wali Allah was born and brought up, and which he so sincerely wanted to reform. All those who have written about him, have acknowledged the tremendous intellectual, scientific, social, spiritual and moral contribution he rendered not only for the welfare of his contemporary society but for the betterment of future generations as well. For example, according to A.S.Bazmee Ansari, "Shah Wali Allah may be called the founder of Islamic modernism. He was much ahead of his times, a revolutionary thinker who attempted, although with little success, the reintegration of the socio-economic and religio-ethical structure of Islam. His chief merit, however, lies in the propagation of the doctrine of *tatbik* (conciliation) which he skilfully applied even to such controversial problems as the *khilafa* and the conflict between dogmatic theology and mysticism".[5]

In his book '*Tajdīd-u-Ihya'ay Dīn*' S. A. Maududi has devoted a whole chapter to the life and works of Shah Wali Allah. He writes: "When one compares his work with his time and atmosphere, one wonders how a man of his vision, thoughts and mentality came into being. Who does not know the India of Farrukh Sayr, Muhammad Shah Rangeela and Shah Alam? In that dark age grows up and rises an independent thinker and visionary (*mubassir*) whose thinking is free and independent of all the restrictions of his time and society. He breaks up centuries' old prejudices and stagnation of traditional (*taqlidi*) science, and investigates every issue of life diligently. He leaves behind such a vast literature, which in its language, style, ideas, thoughts, research materials, and deducted conclusions does not show any effect of his society. And even by going through its pages one cannot assume that these works could have been written in a place which was surrounded by luxury, selfishness, killing and plunder, compulsion and oppression, disorder and anarchy".[6]

When we look at his works we find that Shah Wali Allah did not launch any practical movement for reforming the society, although as a Muslim leader and *Sufi Shaikh* he commanded respect and influence. But this does not mean that he remained aloof from the events of his surroundings. In a statement in *Al-Tafhimat*, he states: "If the circumstances require me to wage war to improve the situation, I am fully capable to do so". But in practice he did not do any such thing, for which he is criticised in comparison to the work of his contemporary Muhammad b.'Abd al-Wahhab.

There could be several explanations. It may be because by his nature he was a great thinker and philosopher. Or it could be that he did not want to create any disturbance, because after all a government was functioning although it was weak and incompetent. Or, it could be that in view of moral, spiritual and social decadence he did not have much confidence in the people to respond to his call.

However, we notice that on several occasions in his writings, and in his correspondence with some of his contemporary rulers like Grand Wazir Asif Jah, Rohaila leader Najeeb al-Dawla and Ahmad Shah Abdali of Afghanistan, he urged them to take action against the anarchists and rebel tribes of Maharattas and Jats. But the responses given by these rulers were hasty, based on short term and temporary solutions and did not have any considerable impact on the situation.

Another serious criticism made against Shah Wali Allah is that although he was a man of great vision who presented revolutionary ideas to reform the society and appealed to some rulers to act against the Maharattas and others, he did not warn against the greater danger posed by the activities of the East India Company, which had by that time established itself in some parts of the country.

Thus, the picture of Shah Wali Allah, which emerges before us, is that of a great thinker, reformer and writer, and who in addition to his intellectual pursuits was also a great *Sufi Shaikh*. He is credited with many books and treatises on different subjects, which depict him as a great scholar, revolutionary thinker and a social scientist.

Here it is not possible to list all his books, but some of his main works are mentioned below.

Fath al-Rahmān bi Tarjuma al-Qur'an: as mentioned above, it is an annotated translation of Qur'an in Persian.

Al-Fawz al-Kabīr fi usul al-Tafsir: it deals with the principles of Qur'anic exegesis.

Al-Musawwa: a commentary on *Muwatta'* of Imam Malik in Arabic.

Al-Musaffa: similar work in Persian.

Hujjat Allah al-Baligha: this book is mainly about the secrets of religion and also deals with metaphysics, politics, finance and political economy.

Al-Budūr al-Bazigha: it deals with various issues of *Tasawwuf.*

Al-'Iqd al-Jīd fi ahkām al-ijtihad wa'l-taqlid: it deals with the issues of *taqlid* and *ijtihad.*

Tafhimat-i Ilahiyya: it contains his addresses to various groups of society such as soldiers and rulers, and points out their faults and weaknesses.

Izalat khafa' 'an khilafat al-Khulafa': as it is evident from the title, in addition to defending the caliphate of Abu Bakr and 'Umar, the book also deals with Islamic political system, principles of economics, *ijtihad* and judicial decisions of 'Umar ibn al-Khattab.

Fuyūd al-Haramayn: it consists on his spiritual observations, meditations and dreams he went through during his stay at Makkah and Madina.

Anfas al-'Ārifin: it comprises his autobiography and events of the lives of his father, uncle and other ancestors and teachers.

Al-Insaf fi bayan sabab al-ikhtilaf: the present work, which deals with the origin, development of *Fiqh* and the causes of difference of opinion among different schools of thought.

It would thus appear that his writings are the main sources for understanding his views and ideas. When one looks at the way he tried to reform the society, it becomes clear that he used different methods and approaches. For example, in *Tafhimat-i-Ilahiyya* he appears as a social scientist and moral preacher. With great courage, confidence and openness he addresses different sections of the society including rulers, *Sufis* and masses. In these addresses, he criticises these people and advises them to adapt themselves to the spirit of Islamic teachings, common sense and humanity.

Here is an example of his addresses to *Sufis*, kings and rulers.

"I say to the descendants of *masha'ikh* (leaders of *Sufism*) who have ascended to their forefathers' seats without any entitlement. What has happened to you? You have created groups and parties and everyone follows his own opinion. You have abandoned the way, which Allah revealed through the tongue of Muhammad (SAAS) and which is mercy, kindness and guidance for the mankind. Everyone amongst you has made himself an Imam. He invites people to himself and considers himself the guide and guided, but he himself is misguided and misleads others. I am not happy with those (*Sufi masha'ikh*) who give discipleship (*bay'ah*) to people in order to accumulate some wealth, or mix up worldly desires with the learning of knowledge.

Oh Kings! In this age it is the will of *mala' a'la* (the exalted assembly of angels) that you keep your swords unsheathed, until Allah does not decide between Muslims and Polytheists, and until rebels, non- believers and the vicious do not join the ranks of those who are weaker than them. When this happens it is the will of *mala' a'la* that you appoint an *amir* (ruler) everywhere at the junction (*manzil*) of three to four days journey and whose job it should be to recuperate the right of the oppressed from the oppressor, implement *hudud* (legal punishment) and try to create peace and harmony among the people.

I say to the rulers, don't you fear Allah. You are relishing enjoyment and have left the citizens to their own fate. The result is that they are exploiting each other. Alcohol is being consumed openly and you don't disapprove of it".

I say one thing to all sections of the Muslim community: "You have been overwhelmed by avarice and greed. The devil has dominated you. Women are confronting men, and men look at women with contempt. You regard *haram* as good and *halal* as bad."[7]

Obviously these passages depict a very grim picture of the Muslim society during the time of Shah Wali Allah. To a reformer like him, who was well versed in Islamic history the causes of this decline were too well known. We notice that he critically examined Islamic history through its different stages. He concluded that transformation of *caliphate* into monarchy and the replacement of *ijtihad* with *taqlid* were the main causes of the decline of Islamic civilisation.

He looked back at the reign of the *pious caliphate* when Islamic institutions were functioning properly and Islamic values prevailed. He says: "In the past (religious) admonition and *fatwa* were conducted in consultation with the Caliph, and no one was allowed to conduct admonition and issue *fatwa*. But after this change (of *caliphate* to monarchy) the issuance of *fatwa* and the delivery of admonition became common practice. And later the condition, that *fatwa* should be issued in consultation with the pious (*'ulama'*) was also revoked".[8]

He found sharp contrast between the rule of *Khulafa' al-Rashidun* and that of his contemporary Muslim rulers who were flagrantly violating the Islamic principles. He therefore found "no difference between the rule of these (so called Muslim rulers) and that of *Majus*. The only difference between them was that they (the former) pray and verbally testify to the article of Faith." He added: "We are born in the shadow of this change and we don't know what has been destined by Allah for the future".[9]

Shah Wali Allah was also very keen on creating unity and some sort of understanding among the Muslims, who were divided bitterly, on sectarian, theological and jurisprudential lines. He felt he was inspired by Allah for this purpose. He writes: "By the grace of Allah all the sciences of this *ummah* have been gathered together in my heart, whether they are *ma'qulat* (works of logic and philosophy), *manqulat* (related to traditional sciences), and whether they are sciences of *wijdan* (intuition) or *kashf* (divine inspiration). Allah has enabled me to reconcile one science with another, and thus the difference therein comes to an end, and everything looks good at its place and there does not remain any contradiction. My principle of *tatbiq* (conciliation) between different and contradictory views covers all fields of knowledge. It includes *Fiqh*, Theology and issues of *Tasawwuf* as well."[10]

Minor differences over the interpretation of secondary matters of *Fiqh* and rivalry between the followers of different *madhahib* were adding fuel to these divisions. For example, should *basmala*[11] be joined or not with *sura al-Fatiha* in prayer, should *'āmīn'* be uttered loudly or silently after *sura al-Fatiha* in congregational prayer, and whether despite their differences over the recitation of *sura al-Fatiha* in prayers, followers of different schools of thought can pray together behind one imam while maintaining their particular methods of praying.

It would appear that perhaps it were these kinds of problems, which urged him to write *Al-Insaf*. In his introductory remarks about the reasons for writing this treatise Shah Wali Allah says that Allah inspired him with a *mīzan* (balance), which enabled him to understand the causes of differences that happened among the Muslims. It also helped him to determine what was right and explain that issue clearly. The second reason, which urged him to write *Al-Insaf*, was an inquiry about the causes of differences among the Companions and Followers[12].

The book critically examines the gradual development of Jurisprudence and the science of *Hadith* from the time of the Prophet (SAAS) until the fifth Islamic century.

The clear, fluent and simple style of the author makes reading of most of the book interesting and appealing. A reader familiar with Arabic literature, especially, Qur'an and *Hadith* can easily understand the language and phrases used in the book. One becomes convinced that the work has been written by a native Arab who seems well versed in its language, literature and grammar. The author discusses various issues and principles, corroborates his views through evidences and examples, and uses reasoning and logic in his arguments.

The book has been fairly interlaced with quotations from Qur'an, *Hadith*, traditions of Companions, Followers and the views of the jurists and other scholars. However, on some occasions, especially when he tries to furnish evidence; or quotes sentences or passages from the books of Jurisprudence; or when he quotes incomplete *Ahadith* and events without explanations; or when he uses some rare and unfamiliar terms, principles or phrases; it becomes difficult for the reader to grasp the full meanings of the text. There one gets the impression that the book was aimed at scholars, especially those conversant with *Tafsir*, *Hadith* and *Fiqh*.

الانصاف فى بيان سبب الاختلاف

Al-Insaf fi bayan sabab al-ikhtilaf
A rational explanation of difference of opinion (in *Fiqh*)

In the name of Allah the most gracious and merciful

Praise be to Allah who sent our master Muhammad (SAAS) to mankind to guide them towards Allah with His permission and as a luminous lamp. Then He inspired the Companions, the Followers and the diligent[13] (*mujtahidīn*) jurists to preserve together the essence of their Prophet's (teachings) until the world is called to an end. This is to complete His favour. He has the power over every thing. I bear witness that there is no god but Allah alone and He has no partner. I (also) bear witness that our master Muhammad is His servant and Messenger after whom there is no Prophet (to come), may Allah bless him, his progeny and the Companions altogether.

To proceed: says the one in need of the mercy of Allah the Kind-Wali Allah b. 'Abd al-Rahim, may Allah al-Mighty complete His favours on both of them here and in the world hereafter: "Once Allah al-Mighty inspired my heart to a *mizan* (scale) which explained to me the cause of every disagreement that happened among the followers (*milla*) of Muhammad (SAAS). With (the help of) this (scale) I can recognise what is right in the sight of Allah and in the sight of His Messenger. It (also) enabled me to explain the cause of disagreements so plainly that there remains no doubt and ambiguity.

Then I was asked about the reasons for disagreement among the Companions and those after them, especially over the laws of *Fiqh*. So I set myself to the task of explaining some of that, which was disclosed to me in that hour commensurating with the extent of the time and the grasp of the questioner. As a result a useful treatise of its kind came about which I call *"Al-Insaf fi bayan sabab al- ikhtilaf "*. For me Allah is sufficient and He is the best disposer of affairs. There is no power and no strength except in Allah the Supreme and Powerful".

The reasons for difference of opinion amongst the Companions and Followers over the *furū'* [14]

Behold that *Fiqh* in the noble time of the Messenger of Allah (SAAS), was not recorded. Neither was the search for laws in those days like the search of these *Fuqaha'*. (This is) because they take pain in establishing the basic principles (*al-arkān*), conditions (*al-shurūt*) and the rules of conduct (*adab*) of everything (so that it could) be distinguished from each other on the basis of its evidence. They hypothesise conditions and then on the basis of those hypothetical conditions, they argue. They define what accepts definition and confine what yields to confinement. These and other things of this kind are of their (own) making.

As for the Messenger of Allah (SAAS), he used to do *wudū* (ablution) while the Companions would see him. They would then copy him without being explained by him that this is a *rukn* and that is an *adab*. And when he (SAAS) used to pray they would see him and pray as they had seen him praying. (Similarly) when he performed *hajj*, people saw him and did as they saw him doing.

This was his (SAAS)'s general practice. He did not explain that obligations (*furūd*) of *wudu* were six or four. Neither did he prescribe that if a man performs *wudu* without observing *muwalāt*[15] (continuity) judgement would be made on the validity or invalidity of his *wudu*. On some occasions, however, he used to explain such things.

The Companions rarely asked him about such things. It is reported on the authority of 'Abd Allah b. 'Abbas (RA d.68/687), as saying: "I have never seen a people better than the Companions of the

Messenger of Allah (SAAS). They did not ask him (about anything) until he passed away except for thirteen questions, all of which are (mentioned) in the Qur'an. These include, "They ask you about the fighting in the sacred month, say fighting in it is a serious (offence)"[16], and "They ask you about menstruation"[17]. He added: "They used to ask questions only about those things which were beneficial for them."

'Abd Allah b.'Umar (RA d.73/692) said: "Don't ask about that which did not happen, because I heard 'Umar ibn al-Khattab (RA d.23/643) cursing the one who asks questions about that which did not happen". Al-Qasim (b. Muhammad b. Abu Bakr al-Siddique) said: "Indeed you ask about (such) things, which we didn't use to ask. You delve into things, which we didn't use to delve in and you ask about things I don't know what they are. Had we known them it wouldn't have been permissible for us to hide them".

It is reported on the authority of 'Umar b. Ishaq as saying: "Certainly the Companions of the Messenger of Allah (SAAS) I met were more than those I missed. (But) I never came across a people who were more lenient in their attitude and less strict than them".

It is reported on the authority of 'Ubada b. Busr al-Kindi, who was asked about a woman who died with a people and did not have a legal guardian (*wali*). (In response) he said: "I have met people who were not as much strict as you are, and who did not use to ask questions like yours". These traditions are related by al-Darimi (d.255/868).

(It was the practice of the Prophet (SAAS, that when) people consulted him over the events[18] (*waqa'i*) he would advise them and pronounce the judgement on cases referred to him. When he would see people doing something good he would commend it and disapprove it if it was a reprehensible action (*munkar*). Whatever legal opinion he gave to an advice seeker, or a judgement he made in a case, or disapproval he showed of a person (for his reprehensible action), it (all) happened in public gatherings.

Similarly, the *Shaykhain* Abu Bakr (d.13/634) and 'Umar (RA), when they didn't have the knowledge of an issue, they would ask the people about the *Hadith* of the Messenger of Allah (SAAS). (Once) Abu Bakr (RA), said: "I did not hear the Messenger of Allah (SAAS) saying something about her, i.e. the grandmother's (share in inheritance)". So he asked the people (if they had heard something from him in this respect). After performing the *Zuhr* prayer he said: "Which one of you has heard the Messenger of Allah (SAAS) saying something about (the share of) grandmother?" Mughira b. Shu'ba (d.50/670) said: "I". Abu Bakr asked him: "What did he say?" Mughira replied: "The Messenger of Allah (SAAS) gave her one sixth (of the inheritance)". Then Abu Bakr asked him: "Does anyone else know that?" Muhammad b. Maslamah[19] (d.43/663) said: "He is right". So Abu Bakr gave her one sixth.

(Or take for example) the story concerning 'Umar's consultation with the people over the[20] *ghurra* and then his retraction (*rujū'*) to the report (narrated) by Mughira. Also his consultation with the people over the epidemic (*waba'*)[21] and then his retraction to the report (narrated) by 'Abd al-Rahman b. 'Awf. Similarly his retraction to the report (narrated) by 'Abd al-Rahman b.'Awf with regard to the story of Magian[22] (*Majus*). (Another example is) the delight of 'Abd Allah b. Mas'ud (d.32/651) over the report (narrated) by Ma'qil b. Yasar when it conformed to his view. (Or for instance) the report concerning the return of Abu Musa (al-Ash'ari d.42/662) from 'Umar's door, then 'Umar's inquiry about the *Hadith*, and Abu Sa'id's[23] (al-Khudri's d.74/693) testimony in his (Abu Musa's) support. These kinds of instances are numerous, well known and reported in the two authentic (books of Bukhari and Muslim) and (other books of) *Sunan*.

In general this was his (SAAS)'s noble practice. Every Companion noticed what Allah facilitated him of his (SAAS) worship, legal advices (*fatawa*) and judicial rulings. And so he remembered it, comprehended it and became familiar with the position of everything through circumstantial evidences (*qara'in*) attached to it. The Companions interpreted some of these (practices) in the sense of permissibility (*ibaha*), some in the sense of desirability (*istihbab*) and some in the sense of abrogation (*naskh*) in view of the signs and circumstantial evidences that were sufficient in their opinion (to make such a judgement). The only criterion for them was the feeling of satisfaction and gratification without considering the methods of reasoning. This is just as you see the *bedouins* understand the purpose of conversation among themselves, and by clear (expression), gesture and indication their hearts are so much delighted that they do not realise (it).

And thus his noble time passed away but they remained on that (same pattern). Then they dispersed in towns and every one of them became a leader of an area. There appeared many events (*waqa''i*), and (jurisprudential) cases (*masa'il*) became subject of discussion. Therefore they were consulted for advice on these (matters) to which each one of them responded according to what he has remembered or inferred. And if he did not find in what he has remembered or inferred to suit the answer, he would exercise *ijtihad* on the basis of his personal opinion. This is how he recognised the *'illa* (reason) upon which the Messenger of Allah (SAAS) based the law in his clear injunctions (*mansusat*). In such circumstances the Companions would search for the law wherever they (could) find it sparing no efforts (in their bid) to conform to the purpose of the Prophet (SAAS) (concerning that rule). It was at this point that a variety of differences occurred among them.

Among these (was the one) that one Companion (might have) heard a ruling or *fatwa* and the other didn't hear it. So the (latter) exercised *ijtihad* (on the basis of his personal opinion) in that (matter).

This happened in a number of ways; one of them was that his *ijtihad* conformed to *Hadith*. An example of this is what has been narrated by al-Nasai' (d.302/914) and others. Accordingly, 'Abd Allah b. Mas'ud was asked about a woman whose husband had died and did not fix her *mahr*[24]. He said: "I didn't see the Messenger of Allah (SAAS) giving judgement over this matter". The people, however, kept on coming to him for a month and urged (him to find the answer). Consequently he exercised his *ijtihad* on the basis of his personal opinion. He ruled that her *mahr* would be (equal to) that of women like her without any reduction or addition, and that she has to observe[25] *'iddah* and was entitled to inheritance. There stood up Ma'qil b. Yasar testifying that the Prophet (SAAS) gave similar ruling about one of their women. Ibn Mas'ud was so much delighted that he had never experienced such a delight ever since (embracing) Islam.

The second (type of differences among the Companions) was that the debate (*munāzara*) took place between the two (Companions). (As a result) the *Hadith* emerged in such a way that in strong probability (*ghālib al-zann*) it seemed acceptable. Consequently one of them would withdraw his *ijtihad* in favour of the narrated (*Hadith*).

An example of this is what the Imams have narrated of Abu Huraira (RA d.59/678). Accordingly, he was of the opinion that if someone gets up in the morning in the state of ritual impurity (*junub*), his fast would not be valid. He held this view until he was told by some of the wives of the Prophet (SAAS) contrary to what he believed, and so he withdrew (his opinion).

Thirdly, the *Hadith* reached him but not in the way that in strong probability it seems acceptable, and so he would not abandon his *ijtihad*. Rather, he would question (the authenticity of) *Hadith*. An example of this is what *Ashab al-Usūl*[26] have reported of Fatima bint Qays. She testified before 'Umar ibn al-Khattab that she was triple divorcee, but the Messenger of Allah (SAAS) granted her neither (the right of) maintenance nor residence. ('Umar) rejected her testimony saying: "I will not abandon the Book of Allah on (the basis of) a woman's statement (whom) we don't know whether she has spoken the truth or lied. She (the divorcee) has the right to maintenance and residence." 'A'isha (RA d.58/677) told Fatima: "Don't you fear Allah, i.e. in (your) statement (that the divorcee is) entitled to neither maintenance nor residence".

Another example (of this type of difference) is the report by *Shaikhain* (Bukhari and Muslim). Accordingly, 'Umar ibn al-Khattab was of the opinion that for a (ritually) impure person who does not find water, *tayammum* (substitute to ablution) does not suffice. In response 'Ammar told him that (once) he was travelling with the

Al-Insaf fi bayan sabab al-ikhtilaf

Messenger of Allah (SAAS) that he became ritually impure and did not find the water, so he rubbed the dust all over his body. He then mentioned this to the Messenger of Allah (SAAS). The Messenger of Allah (SAAS) said that it would have sufficed him to have done like this, tapping the ground with his hands and then rubbing with them his face and hands (arms). 'Umar, however, did not accept (the *Hadith*), because the evidence in his opinion could not be substantiated because of a hidden defect he found therein. (This view remained prevalent) until the *Hadith* became widespread in the second generation through many lines of transmission (*turuq*) and the defect (in the meantime) vanished. And so the *Hadith* was (consequently) accepted.

Fourthly, the *Hadith* did not reach him at all. An example of this is what (Imam) Muslim (d.282/895) has reported that ('Abd Allah) b. 'Umar used to ask women to untangle their hairs when they bathe. When 'A'isha (RA) heard that, she said: "How strange it is of Ibn 'Umar to ask women to untangle their hairs. Why doesn't he ask them to shave their heads? Indeed I and the Messenger of Allah (SAAS) used to bathe with one vessel, which I would not pour it out over my head more than three times".

Another example (of such differences) is what has been mentioned by (Muhammad b. Muslim al-Shihab) al-Zuhri (d.124/741). Accordingly, Hind had not known the concession (*rukhsa*) (given) by the Messenger of Allah (SAAS) to the menstruating (*mustahada*). Therefore she used to cry for not praying (during the period of her menstruation).

Among those kinds (of differences was also the one) that they saw the Messenger of Allah (SAAS) doing something, but then some of them interpreted it in the sense of nearness (*qurba*) and some in the sense of permissibility (*ibaha*). An example of this is what has been reported by *Ashab al-Usul* in respect of the question of *al-tahsib*-i.e. stopover at *al-abtah* (valley) during *al-nafar*[27]. The Messenger of Allah (SAAS) stopped there. Abu Huraira and Ibn 'Umar construed this (stopover) in the sense of nearness and treated it as *Sunnah* of *hajj*, while 'A'isha and Ibn 'Abbas considered this (stopover) a (mere) coincidence and not a *Sunnah*.

Another example (of this phenomenon) is the majority view that *ramal*[28] in *tawaf* (circumambulation of the Ka'ba) is *Sunnah*. Ibn 'Abbas, however, believed that it was done by the Prophet (SAAS) as a coincidence in response to an incident. And that was the (taunting) remarks by the polytheists that the fever of Yathrib (Madina) had weakened the Muslims. (Therefore in his opinion *ramal* was) not a *Sunnah*.

Among these (kinds of differences) was (also) the difference of assumption (*al-wahm*) in interpretation. For example, the Messenger of Allah (SAAS) performed *hajj* and was seen by (many) people. Some of them thought that he was *Mutamatti'*[29], some considered him *Quārin*[30], others thought he was *Mufrid*[31].

Another example (of this kind is the one) reported by Abu Dawud (al-Sijistani d.275/910) on the authority of Sa'id b. Jubair (d.95/713). He said: "I told 'Abd Allah b. 'Abbas that I was astonished at the (degree) of disagreement among the Companions of the Messenger of Allah (SAAS) over the *ihlal*[32] of the Messenger of Allah (SAAS) when he put on *ihram* for *hajj* and performed the necessary acts of *ihram*". In response,'Abd Allah b.'Abbas said: "I know better about that. Truly it was the only pilgrimage of the Messenger of Allah (SAAS) and from there arose disagreement among them".

The Messenger of Allah (SAAS) set out for *hajj*. After performing the two *rak'at* prayer in Dh'ul-Hulaifa Mosque he put on *ihram* in the same place and uttered *talbiyah*[33] for *hajj*. After completing his two *rak'at* prayer, many people heard him saying that and remembered it. Then he embarked upon his journey and when his she-camel lifted him up he uttered *talbiyah*, and many people saw that. This is because people were coming (to him) in groups and so they heard him uttering *talbiyah* when his she-camel lifted him up, hence they said: "Surely the Messenger of Allah (SAAS) uttered *talbiyah* when his she-camel lifted him up". Then he continued his journey. When he ascended the top of the steep he uttered *talbiyah* and many people noticed that. So they said: "Indeed he uttered *talbiyah* only when he ascended the top of the steep". By Allah indeed he put on *ihram* and performed the necessary acts of *ihram* at his *musallah* and uttered *talbiyah* when his she-camel lifted him up, and he uttered *talbiyah* when he ascended the top of the steep".

These (differences also) took place because of the difference of inattentiveness and forgetfulness. An example of this is the report that Ibn 'Umar used to say: "The Messenger of Allah (SAAS) performed *'umra* in Rajab". When 'A'isha heard this, she ruled inattentiveness on his part.

These (differences also include) the difference of accurate understanding and retention (*dabt*). An example of this is what Ibn 'Umar or 'Umar reported from the Prophet (SAAS) that the dead person is chastised because of the wailing of his family over him. 'A'isha ruled that he did not perceive the *Hadith* in its context. "(Once) the Messenger of Allah (SAAS) was passing by (the grave of) a Jewess that he found her family wailing over her. There he said: "They are wailing for her while she is being chastised in her grave". Hence he (Ibn 'Umar or 'Umar) considered chastisement a cause of bewailing and thought the rule was generally applicable to every dead person.

Among (these kinds of differences) was (also) their disagreement over (the interpretation of) the cause of rule. An example of this is the (observance of) standing for funeral (procession). Some said this was to show respect for angles and therefore would include believer and non-believer alike. Others said it was because of the horror of death and would therefore include both of them. Hasan b. 'Ali (RA d. 50/669), however, said: "(Once) a funeral procession of a Jew was passing by the Messenger of Allah (SAAS) that he stood up out of his dislike lest it pass over his head". Hence (this rule) specifically applies to non-believer.[34]

These (differences also) include their disagreement over reconciliation between the two contradictory (or inconsistent) *Ahadith* (*al-jam' bayn al-mukhtalifain*). For example, the Messenger of Allah (SAAS) allowed *mut'a* (temporary marriage) during the year of (the conquest of) Khaybar. He allowed it (again) in the year of *Awtas*[35], and then he prohibited it. 'Abd Allah b. 'Abbas said: "The permission was (given) out of necessity and the prohibition (was made) in view of the cessation of necessity and (therefore) the law remains effective in that (final) form". The majority (of scholars), however, said: "The permission was (given) in the sense of permissibility and prohibition (was made) for its abrogation".

(Here is) another example (of this phenomenon). The Messenger of Allah (SAAS) prohibited from facing the *qiblah* (*Ka'ba*) during *istinja'*. A group of people believed in the generality (*'umūm*) of this rule, and that it was not abrogated. One year before he (SAAS) passed away, Jabir (RA) saw him facing the *qibla* while urinating so he thought it an abrogation of previous prohibition. And (once) Ibn 'Umar (RA) saw him (SAAS) answering the call of nature while he was backing towards the *qibla* and facing to Syria, therefore, he rejected their (above-mentioned) view.

A group (of scholars), however, reconciled between the two reports. Al- Sha'bi and others thought the prohibition was (specifically) related to the desert and that in lavatories there was no harm in facing and backing to (*Ka'ba*). Another group believed the statement (of the Prophet (SAAS) was general and definite (*'am muhkam*) and that the action (of the Prophet (SAAS) has the likelihood of being specific to the Prophet (SAAS) and therefore does not stand to be either abrogator or a specific matter (*mukhassas*).

In general the views (*madhahib*) of the Companions of the Prophet (SAAS) became divergent and so the Followers learned from them whatever it was possible for them. As a result they remembered and comprehended whatever they heard of the *Hadith* of the Messenger of Allah (SAAS) and the views of the Companions. They reconciled between *al-mukhtalifat* (contradictory or inconsistent *Ahadith*) as much as it was possible for them. They also gave preference to some of the views (of the Companions) over others. Some of these views became less significant in their opinion even though they were reported on the authority of great Companions such as the reported view of Ibn 'Umar and Ibn Mas'ud about (the validity of) *tayammum* for (ritually) impure person. This view became weak when the *Ahadith* transmitted by 'Ammar, 'Imran b. Husain (d.52/672) and others gained widespread currency.

By that time every scholar among the Followers had (developed) his own *madhhab*. Consequently in every town an Imam was appointed. For example in Madina Sa'id b. al-Musayyab (d.93AH/711AD) and Salim b.'Abd Allah b.'Umar who were succeeded by al-Zuhri, Qadi Yahya b. Sa'id and Rabi'a b. Abu 'Abd al-Rahman (d.136AH/753AD); in Makkah 'Ata b. Abi Rabah (d.114AH/732AD), in Kufa Ibrahim al-Nakh'i (d.95AH/713AD) and al-Sha'bi ('Amir b. Shrahil d.103AH/721AD); in Basra Hasan al-Basri (d.110AH/728AD); in Yemen Ta'us b. Kaysan and in Syria Makhul (al-Shami d.118AH/736AD). Allah made people's hearts thirsty of their knowledge and they craved for it. From these scholars people learned *Ahadith, fatawa* and the views of the Companions, as well as the *madhahib* and investigations (developed) by these scholars themselves.

People used to consult them for advice on legal matters and (thus) discussion on (such) issues became rotating among them. (As a result) disputes were referred to them (for solutions). Sa'id b. al-Musayyab, Ibrahim al-Nakh'i and people like them had collected the entire sections of *Fiqh*. In every field of *Fiqh* they had principles, which they had acquired from the predecessors.

Sa'id and his companions were of the opinion that the people of *Haramayn* were the most reliable in *Fiqh*. The basis of their *madhhab* were the *fatawa* of 'Umar and 'Uthman (RA), and their legal decisions, and the *fatawa* of 'Abd Allah b. 'Umar, 'A'isha and Ibn 'Abbas (RA), and the legal decisions of the judges of Madina.

Out of all that they collected whatever Allah facilitated them. They examined it with a view of consideration and scrutiny. Of this whatever was agreed upon among the scholars of Madina they would adhere to it firmly, and on whatever there was disagreement among them they would accept (that view which was) the strongest and the most preferable. (The strength and preference of a view depended on the fact) that either because this was the opinion of the majority or because it was in concordance with a strong analogy or clear deduction of the Book (of Allah) and the *Sunnah* (of the Prophet (SAAS) and so on. And if they did not find the answer to the question in what they had collected from them (the '*ulama*' of Madina), then they would deduce from their (*salaf*'s) statement and search for the signs (*al-īma'*) and alluded meanings (*al-iqtida'*) (in the text). Thus they developed a collection of many *masa'il* in every field (of *Fiqh*).

Ibrahim (al-Nakh'i) and his companions were of the opinion that 'Abd Allah b. Mas'ud (RA) and his companions were the most reliable in *Fiqh*. This is just as 'Alqama said to Masruq (b. 'Abd al-Rahman al-Ajda' al-Hamdani d.62AH/681AD): "Is there anyone among the Companions more reliable (in *Fiqh*) than 'Abd Allah (b. Mas'ud)?" And Abu Hanifa (RA)'s (d.150AH/767AD) remarks to al-Auza'i ('Abd al-Rahman d.157AH/773AD): "Ibrahim is more knowledgeable than Salim (b.'Abd Allah b. 'Umar). If it were not for the excellence of Companionship, I would have said that 'Alqama is more knowledgeable than 'Abd Allah b.'Umar". And 'Abd Allah (ibn 'Umar) is (too well known).

Ibrahim's school of thought is based on the *fatawa* of 'Abd Allah b. Mas'ud and the legal decisions of 'Ali (b. Abi Talib RA) (d.40AH/660AD), and the decisions of Shuraih and other judges of Kufa. From all this he collected what Allah facilitated him and then he treated their traditions[36] (*āthār*) just as the people of Madina treated the traditions of their (scholars). Then he deduced the way they deduced, and this is how he developed a collection of many *masa'il* in every field of *Fiqh*.

Sa'id b. al-Musayyab was the spokesman of the jurists of Madina. He was the best of them at remembering the legal decisions of 'Umar and the *Ahadith* (reported) by Abu Huraira (RA). On the other hand, Ibrahim was the spokesman of the jurists of Kufa. Whenever they both spoke about something and did not attribute it to anyone, it was mostly (understood to be) attributed to one of the ancestors either expressly or by way of indication and other things like that. Then the jurists of their respective cities would agree on it, adhere to both of them, comprehend it and make deduction on the basis of it, and Allah knows best.

The reasons for difference of opinion (*madhhab*) among the *Fuqaha'*

Behold that after the period of Followers Allah created a new generation of *bearers of knowledge*. This was a (sign of) fulfilment of what He promised the Messenger of Allah (SAAS), since he (SAAS) said: " From every (coming) generation just and fair people will carry this knowledge". So from those who met him (SAAS) people learnt the method of *wudu, ghusl, salah, hajj, nikah*, sales and the rest of that which happens frequently. They narrated *Ahadith* of the Prophet (SAAS), heard the legal decisions of the judges of the country and *fatawa* of their *muftis*[37], inquired about the *masa'il* and exercised *ijtihad* with regard to all these (matters). Then they became the leaders of the community and were entrusted with the affairs (of responsibility). They followed the pattern of their teachers and spared no effort in search for the signs and alluded meanings of the text. They made legal decisions, gave *fatawa*, narrated (*Ahadith*) and became involved in teaching. The work of the *'ulama'* of this generation was identical.

The end result of their work was to adhere to all *musnad*[38] and *mursal*[39] *Ahadith* of the Messenger of Allah (SAAS) and to infer from the views of the Companions and Followers. (This attitude was based) on their understanding that these were the transmitted *Ahadith* of the Messenger of Allah (SAAS) (but were) considered less significant by the Companions and therefore the Followers treated them[40] *mawqufa*. This is exactly what Ibrahim (al-Nakh'i) said. After narrating the *Hadith* concerning the prohibition of *muhaqala*[41] and *muzabana*[42] by the Messenger of Allah (SAAS), he was asked: "Don't you remember any other *Hadith* of the Messenger of Allah (SAAS)?" He replied: "Yes indeed! But to say, 'Abd Allah said, 'Alqama said, is dearer to me".

Al-Sha'bi was asked similar question when his opinion was sought about a *marfū' Hadith*.[43] He replied: "No. But (to ascribe the statement) to someone other the Prophet (SAAS) is dearer to us, because if there is any addition or deficiency therein, (the burden of responsibility) would lie on someone other than the Prophet

(SAAS)".

Or (the end result of their work) was to adhere to the views of the Companions and Followers) on this understanding that these views were either inferences (*istinbat*) from *al-mansūs* (the textual injunctions of Qur'an or *Hadith*) or (these views were the result of their effort) of *ijtihad* based on their opinion. In all these matters the work of Companions and Followers was better than those who were to come after them. This is because they were more sound (in judgement), advanced in age and more receptive to learning. This is how practice on *Hadith* was determined unless there was disagreement among themselves and (also if) the *Hadith* of the Messenger of Allah (SAAS) openly opposed their view.

(It was also the end result of their work) to refer to the views of the Companions if there was disagreement among the *Ahadith* of the Messenger of Allah (SAAS) over a *mas'ala*. If they spoke of abrogation of some of these (*Ahadith*) or suggested its interpretation instead of taking it in its literal sense or they did not speak about it clearly, but agreed on abandoning it and not acting on its contents. (All these factors) would have been treated as if there was a cause of defiencey therein, or a verdict on its abrogation or that it was open for interpretation. (In all such circumstances) they used to follow them (Companions). This has been the view of Malik (b. Anas d.179AH/795AD) (which he expressed) concerning the *Hadith wulūgh al-kalb*[44]. (He said): "This *Hadith* did appear but I don't know what is its actual position". According to Ibn al-Hajib (Jamal al-Din Abu 'Amr 'Uthman b.'Umar b. Abu Bakr al-Maliki d.646AH/1249AD) in *Mukhtasar al- (Muntahā' fi'l-Usūl*) it means that I have not seen the jurists acting on it.

(And thirdly) when there was difference of opinion among the Companions and Followers over an issue then the preferred option for every scholar would be (to adhere to) the *madhhab* of the people of his town and *shuyukh* (teachers of *Hadith*). This is because he knows better (which one of) their statements are genuine (and which one) faulty and (he is also) well aware of those principles (which are) suitable (to be applied) to those (statements). And (also because) his heart is more inclined towards their excellence and erudition.

Therefore the *madhhab* of 'Umar, 'Uthman, 'A'isha, Ibn 'Umar, Ibn 'Abbas and Zaid b. Thabit (RA d.45AH/665AD) and their companions like Sa'id b. al-Musayyab, who was the most learned among them of the legal decisions of 'Umar and the *Ahadith* (reported by) Abu Huraira (d. 59AH/678AD); and like 'Urwa (b. Zubair b. al-'Awwam (d. 94AH/712AD), Salim (d.106AH/724AD), 'Ikrima (client of Ibn 'Abbas (d.105AH/723AD), 'Ata b. Yasar, Qasim, 'Ubaid Allah b. 'Abd Allah, al-Zuhri, Yahya b. Sa'id, Zaid b. Aslam (d.136AH/753AD) and Rabi'a (b. Farrukh al-Taimi d.136AH/753AD), (the *madhhab* of all the above mentioned) in view of the people of Madina is more worthy of adherence than others. This is in view of what the Prophet (SAAS) has described the virtues of Madina, and also because in every age it has been the abode of the jurists and the meeting point of scholars. That is why you would see Malik insisting on adherence to their view because it is well known of him that he used to adhere to the consensus of the people of Madina. Bukhari has devoted a chapter on adherence to what the (scholars) of *Haramayn* had agreed.

In view of the people of Kufa the *madhhab* of 'Abd Allah b. Mas'ud (RA) and his companions, and the legal decisions of al-Shuraih, al-Sha'bi and the *fatawa* of Ibrahim are more worthy of adherence than others. And this was the viewpoint of 'Alqama. When Masruq turned to the view of Zaid b. Thabit with regard to *tashrik*[45] he ('Alqama) said: "Is anyone among you more reliable than 'Abd Allah b. Mas'ud?" He (Masruq) replied: "No, but I saw Zaid b. Thabit and the people of Madina practising *tashrik*". So if the inhabitants of a town agree on something they would stick to it firmly.

This is similar to the position of Malik, who said: "The *Sunnah*, which is not disputed in our view, is so and so". Hence if the people of a town disagreed they would accept the strongest and most preferred *Hadith* as it was when supported by many people or because of its concordance with a strong analogy or deduction based on Qur'an and *Sunnah* (of the Prophet (SAAS). With regard to similar position Malik said: "This is the best of what I heard".

If they did not find the answer to the question in what they have learned from them (Companions and Followers) then they would deduce from their statement and search for signs and alluded meanings in the text.

The people of this generation were inspired to recording (*tadwīn*). Malik and Muhammad b.'Abd al-Rahman b. Abu Dhi'b (d.158AH/774AD) recorded in Madina. Ibn Juraij ('Abd al-Malik b.'Abd al-'Aziz d.150AH/767AD) and Ibn 'Uyayna (Sufyan d.198AH/813AD) recorded at Makka. Al-Thawri (Sufyan b. Sa'id al-Kufi d.161AH/777AD) recorded in Kufa and Rabi' b. al-Sabih (al-Sa'di d.160AH/776AD) recorded at Basra. They all followed this method already mentioned.

After performing the *hajj*, the 'Abbasid Caliph Mansur (d.169AH/775AD) said to Malik: "I have decided to order that your books be copied and sent to all the major Muslims cities, asking them to act upon them exclusively". Malik said: "O Commander of the Faithful! Don't do this, because the people have already received the views of the Companions, heard the *Ahadith* and narrated the reports. Each group adheres to what has been already passed on to it. They have been informed of the difference of opinion among the Companions and Followers; so let them have what people of every town had chosen for themselves.

According to another report the story is related to Harun al-Rashid (d.193AH/809AD). He asked Malik as if he could hang his *Muwatta* in *Ka'ba* and urge the people to act upon it. Malik replied: "Don't do that, because the Companions of the Messenger of Allah (SAAS) had differences over the *furu'*. They had dispersed in the country, and despite their differences every *Sunnah* has been acted upon". Harun said: "O Abu 'Abd Allah! May Allah bless you with success". This is reported by al-Suyuti (Jalal al-Din d. 911AH/1505AD).

Malik was the most reliable among all the Madinians who reported the *Hadith* from the Messenger of Allah (SAAS). He was the most authentic in *isnad*[46] and the most learned in the legal decisions of 'Umar and the views of 'Abd Allah b. 'Umar, 'A'isha (RA) and their companions from the Seven Jurists[47]. It was Malik and people like him with whose (help) *'Ilm al-Riwaya* (the 'Science of

Transmission of *Hadith*) and *fatwa* became established. When he became in charge of the affairs, he narrated *Ahadith*, gave *fatwa*, benefited (others) and well utilised his knowledge. It is he to whom fits the saying of the Prophet (SAAS): "Very soon a time will come that people will make long journeys on camels in quest of knowledge but they will not find anyone more learned than a scholar of Madina". This is according to what Ibn 'Uyanah and 'Abd al-Razzaq have reported, and their statement is itself a testimony.

Then his companions collected his reports and selected views. They abridged them and scrutinised them, wrote commentaries on them and made deductions on their basis. They discussed the principles and evidences of his views. (Then) they dispersed in the North West Africa and (other) parts of the world, and through them Allah benefited most of His creature. If you want to know the actual position of what we have said about the origin of his *madhhab* then look into (his) book, *al-Muwatta*, where you will find exactly what we have mentioned.

Abu Hanifa (al-Nu'man b. Thabit d.150AH/767AD) was the staunchest adherent of the *madhhab* of Ibrahim al-Nakh'i and his companions. Very rarely did he overstep him. He was highly competent in deducing (the issues) from the *madhhab* of Ibrahim and was well versed in the methods of deductions. He devoted his full attention to the *furū'*. And if you wish to know the actual position of what we have said then sum up the views of Ibrahim and his colleagues from *Kitab al-Āthār* of Muhammad (b. al-Hasan al-Shaibani d.189AH/805AD) *may Allah have mercy on him*, *Jamī'* of 'Abd al-Razzaq and *Musannaf* of Abu Bakr b. Abi Shaiba. Then compare them with the *madhhab* of Abu Hanifa. You will notice that except for a very few places it does not differ from that method, and even in that small proportion it does not deviate from the views held by the *Fuqaha'* of Kufa.

Among his companions Abu Yusuf (d.182AH/795AD), *may Allah have mercy on him,* was the most renowned one. He assumed the office of the Chief Justice during the reign of Harun al-Rashid and that was the reason for the promotion of his *madhhab* and the administration of its laws in the regions of 'Iraq, Khurasan, and Transoxiana.

And the most excellent among them in writing and the most keen on learning and teaching was Muhammad b. al-Hasan (al-Shaibani d.189AH/805AD). He is known to have studied (*Fiqh*) under Abu Hanifa and Abu Yusuf and then went to Madina where he studied *Muwatta* under Malik. Then he examined his position and compared the *madhhab* of his companions case by case with *Muwatta*. If he found therein concurrence then it was all right, otherwise he would see if a group of Companions and Followers held similar views as those of his companions. (If he found concurrence) then it (too) was acceptable. (But) if (in the practice of his companions) he found a weak analogy (*qiyas da'if*) or a lenient deduction (*takhrij layyin*) opposed by a sound *Hadith* on which the *Fuqaha'* have acted or the practice of the majority of *'ulama* contradict that (analogy or deduction), (then) he would abandon it in favour of one of the *madhahib* of *salaf* which seemed most preferable (*arjah*) to him at that time.

As far as it was possible for both of them (Abu Yusuf and Muhammad), they always practised the method of Ibrahim and his colleagues just as Abu Hanifa used to do. Their disagreement was only over one of the two things; either their *shaikh* (Abu Hanifa) had a deduction in accordance with the *madhhab* of Ibrahim in which they opposed him, or there were different views of Ibrahim and people of his stature on which they (both) differed with their *shaikh*. And this difference was over giving preference to some of these views over others.

(Imam) Muhammad, *may Allah have mercy on him*, wrote (books) in which he compiled the views of all three of them and which benefited many people. As a result these writings became the focus of attention of Abu Hanifa's companions. They abridged them and presented them in understandable way. (Some of them) wrote commentaries on these books, (others used them) for deduction or for establishing the origins of their principles or for corroborating (from these principles). Then they dispersed to Khurasan and Transoxina and that is (what is) called the *madhhab* of Abu Hanifa. Yet the *madhhab* of Abu Hanifa together with the *madhhab* of Abu Yusuf and Muhammad is regarded as one despite the fact that they both (Abu Yusuf and Muhammad) were[48] *mujtahid mutlaq*. Their disagreement (with him) in *usul* and *furu'* was quite significant, but in view of their congruence in this principle and because of the fact that their *madhahib* were recorded together in *al-Mabsūt* and *al-Jāmi' al-Kabīr*, (the *madhhab* of all three is regarded as one).

(Muhammad b. Idris) al-Shafi'i (d. 204AH/819AD) appeared during the early days of the emergence of the two *madhahib* (of Abu Hanifa and Malik) and whilst their *usul* and *furu'* were being arranged. He examined the work of predecessors and found therein matters (which) held back his reign from following their path. These are mentioned in the beginning of (his) *Kitab al-Umm*.

One of them was that he found the *Fuqaha'* acting upon *mursal* and *munqati'*[49] (*Ahadith*) which caused defect therein. This is because when the lines of transmission (*turuq*) of *Hadith* are brought together, it would appear that many a *mursal* have no origin and many a *mursal* are at variance with *musnad*. Therefore he decided not to act on *mursal* but only if it fulfils certain conditions which are mentioned in books of *Usul* (*al-Fiqh*).

(Secondly he found) that (in past) the rules of reconciliation between *al-mukhtalifat* (contradictory or inconsistent *Ahadith*) were not precisely defined which used to cause defect in (the outcome of) their independent judgement. Hence he laid down its principles and recorded them in (a) book, and this was the first compilation in *Usūl al-Fiqh*.

An example of this (phenomenon is the report that) has reached us. Accordingly, (once) Shafi'i called on Muhammad b. al-Hasan (al-Shaibani) while he was criticising the people of Madina for giving judgement on the basis of single witness on oath (*al-shahid al-wahid ma'al-yamīn*). He maintained that this was an addition to the Book of Allah. Shafi'i asked him: "Have you proved that addition to the Book of Allah on the basis of *khabar wahid*[50] is not permissible?" The latter replied: "Yes!" Shafi'i asked him: "Why do you say that inheritor is not allowed to make a will in view of the saying (of the

Prophet) (SAAS): "Truly there is no (right of) bequest for an heir", while al-Mighty Allah has said: "It is prescribed upon you, when death approaches you to make a will"[51]. Then he cited (other) examples of this kind against him, which brought an end to the argument of Muhammad b. al-Hasan.

(Thirdly) some of the sound *Ahadith* did not reach the scholars among the Followers (who were) given the charge of *fatwa*. So they exercised *ijtihad* on the basis of their opinions, or followed general guidelines, or followed those Companions who had passed away, and gave *fatwa* accordingly. Then (these sound *Ahadith*) appeared in the third generation but they did not act[52] upon them on the assumption that they contradict the practice of the people of their town and their tradition over which there was no disagreement among them. Hence in their view, this was a default in the *Hadith* and a cause for its annulment.

Or (these sound *Ahadith*) did not appear in the third generation but appeared afterwards. This happened when the scholars of *Hadith* closely examined the (process of) collecting the chains of *Hadith*. (In pursuit of this they) travelled to (different) parts of (Muslim) land and searched for *bearers of knowledge*. As a result there appeared in great number such *Ahadith*, which were reported only by one or two Companions and from whom only one or two men had transmitted such *Ahadith*. This is why they remained unknown to the scholars of *Fiqh*.

Most of the *Ahadith* appeared during the period of *huffaz*[53] (who were) collectors of *turuq* (lines of transmission) of many *Ahadith*, which were for example reported by the people of Basra, while the rest of the regions were unaware of them.

Shafi'i maintained that the *'ulama'* among the Companions and Followers always looked for *Hadith* over an issue, and if they did not find one they would adhere to another type of reasoning. Later if the *Hadith* appeared to them they would withdraw their *ijtihad* in favour of *Hadith*. If that were the case then their non-adherence to a *Hadith* would not be (assumed) a fault therein, unless they explained the

Al-Insaf fi bayan sabab al-ikhtilaf

cause of the fault (*al-'illa al-qadiha*).

An example of this phenomenon is the *Hadith al-Qullatain* [54]. It is truly a sound *Hadith* transmitted through many *turuq*. Most of these *turuq* go back to Walid b. Kathir (who reported it) from Muhammad b. Ja'far b. Zubair (who reported it) from 'Abd Allah. Or (they are traced back from) Muhammad b. 'Abbad b. Ja'far- from 'Ubaid Allah b.'Abd Allah who both (reported it) from Ibn 'Umar. The chains, then became diverse and ramified. Although Muhammad b.'Abbad and 'Ubaid Allah b. 'Abd Allah were reliable (narrators), they did not issue *fatwa* and people did not rely on them (for advice). Similarly, the *Hadith* (*al-Qullatain*) did not appear during the period of Sa'id b. al-Musayyab or during the period of al-Zuhri. Hence it was not considered or acted upon by Hanafis or by Malikis. However Shafi'i did act upon it.

Another example was the[55] *Hadith Khiyār al-Majlis*. It is a sound *Hadith* transmitted through many *turuq* and acted upon by the Prophet's Companions Ibn 'Umar and Abu Huraira (RA). However, it was not known to the Seven Jurists and their contemporaries, and so was not talked about. Malik and Abu Hanifa considered this a cause of defect in the *Hadith*, although Shafi'i acted upon it.

Fourthly the views of the Companions were collected during the period of Shafi'i, and therefore became available in abundance. However they were diverse and ramified. Shafi'i found most of these (views) contradicted the sound *Hadith* as it did not reach the (Companions). He found that in such situations the predecessors always used to refer to *Hadith*. Therefore he stopped adhering to their (Companions') views unless they agreed, saying: "They were men, and we are (also) men (like them)".

(Fifthly), Shafi'i saw that a group of *Fuqaha'* mix up *al-ra'i*[56] which has[57] not been allowed by the *Shari'a*, with analogy (*qiyas*) which has been confirmed by it, thus not distinguishing one from another. Sometimes they call *ra'i*, *istihsan*.[58] And by *al-ra'i* I mean to establish it as a cause of a rule in a difficulty (*mazinna haraj*) or where an interest (*maslaha*) is involved. While *qiyas* means to deduce *'illa* from (clearly) defined law (*al-hukm al-mansūs*), and so that the

41

law is based on (the same *'illa*). Thus he completely invalidated this category (of *al-ra'i*) saying: "Whoever applies *istihsan* (actually) wants to be the *Law Giver*". This is reported by Ibn al-Hajib in *Sharh Mukhtasar al-Usūl*.

For example the maturity (age) of orphan is an unclear matter. So in its place the *Fuqaha'* set up the right sense (*rushd*) and that is (when the orphan) reaches (the age of) twenty-five years. They said: "When the orphan reaches this age his property should be handed over to him". They maintained that this was *istihsan,* while *qiyas* suggests that it should not be handed over to him.

In short when Shafi'i saw such things in the work of predecessors, he began work on *Fiqh* from its basics. So he established its *usūl* and branched out their *furū'*. He produced excellent and useful books. The *Fuqaha'* gathered around him and engaged themselves in abridgement, explanation, inference and deduction (of his views) and then they dispersed to (different parts of) the country. This is (how) the *madhhab* of Shafi'i (was developed), and Allah knows best.

The reasons for differences between Ashab al-Hadith and Ashab al-Ra'i

Behold that during the period of Sa'id b. al-Musayyab, Ibrahim and al-Zuhri, and during the period of Malik and Sufyan, and (even) after them, there were people among the *'ulama'* who did not like getting involved (and giving) independent opinion (*al-ra'i*) (on matters of *Shari'a*). They were afraid of issuing *fatwa* and inferring (*istinbat*) except in circumstances, which were unavoidable. They were mainly concerned with the reporting of *Hadith* of the Messenger of Allah (SAAS).

(Once) 'Abd Allah b. Mas'ud was asked about something, (to which) he responded: "I dislike making something lawful (*halal*) for you which Allah has made unlawful (*haram*) for you or making unlawful that which Allah has made lawful for you".

Mu'adh b. Jabal (RA) said: "O People! Don't hasten to the trial before it descends, because among the Muslims there are always some people who when asked about something they begin explaining it in detail". Similar (view) has been reported of 'Umar, 'Ali, Ibn 'Abbas and Ibn Mas'ud (RA) with regard to their dislike of maintaining something that had not been revealed.

Ibn 'Umar, (RA*)*, said to Jabir b. Zaid (al-Azdi d. 93AH/711AD): "You belong to the *Fuqaha'* of Basra, only give *fatwa* on the basis of clear (expression) of Qur'an and the established *Sunnah*, because if you do (something) other than that you will destroy yourself and (others)".

Abu'l-Nasr says: "When Abu Salama came to Basra, Hasan (al-Basri) and I went to see him. He asked Hasan: "Are you Hasan? No one in Basra is dearer to me than seeing you, and that is because I have been told that you give *fatwa* on the basis of your own opinion. Don't give *fatwa* on the basis of your own *ra'i*. Give *fatwa* only if it is on the basis of the *Sunnah* of the Messenger of Allah (SAAS) or the Revealed Book".

(Muhammad) b. al-Munkadir (d.130AH/747AD) said: "The scholar steps into what is between Allah and His servants, therefore he should find his way out (as well)".

Al-Shaʻbi was asked: "What did you do when you were asked about something?" He replied: "You have come to the (right) person (who is) familiar with the matter. (Usually) when the man was asked (about something) he would refer it to his colleague, saying: "Give them *fatwa*", and the question will remain (rotating) until it would come back to the first one".

Al-Shaʻbi said: "Take what they relate to you from the Messenger of Allah (SAAS), and throw in rubbish what they tell you of their own opinion". These traditions, including the last one, are related by al-Darimi.

Consequently the recording of *Hadith* and *āthār*, and the writing of books and transcripts became quite widespread in Islamic countries. It was rare for a narrator not to record (*Hadith*), or write a book or (have) a copy, as this became one of their main preoccupations. The great men who witnessed that period travelled around the cities of Hijaz, Syria, ʻIraq, Egypt, Yemen and Khurasan, (where) they collected the books and searched for transcripts. They made penetrating search about *Gharib*[59] *Hadith* and rare *athar*.

As a result of their interest and efforts more *Ahadith* and *athar* were collected than by any one before, and (more things) became available to them, than had been available to any one before. The *turuq* (chains) of *Ahadith* were so abundant that the number of chains of *Ahadith* in their possession exceeded hundred or more. As a result some of the chains uncovered what was hidden by some others. The (traditionists) recognised the position of every *Hadith* from the point of view of (its) *gharaba* (peculiarity because of single narrator) and (*istifada*) widespread circulation which enabled them to closely examine the *mutabaʻat*[60] and *shawahid*. As a result many sound *Ahadith* came to their knowledge, which were previously unknown to those involved with *fatwa*.

Shafiʼi said to Ahmad (b. Hanbal) (d.241AH/855AD): "You know more than us about sound *Ahadith*, so if there is a sound *Hadith* (with someone), let me know so that I can visit him whether he is a Kufi, Basri or Shami". This is reported by Ibn al-Humam. This (concern of Shafi'i) is due to (the fact) that a number of sound *Ahadith* are reported only by the people of a particular city, such as *afrad*[61] (individual) Syrians or 'Iraqis. Or (they were reported by) members of a particular family such as the *nuskha* of Burayd (transmitted) from Abu Burda (who reported it) from Abu Musa (al-Ash'ari). Similarly the *nuskha* of 'Amr ibn Shu'aib (d.118AH/736AD) (who reported it) from his father (and he) from his grandfather.

Or (these sound *Ahadith* were reported by such) a Companion who was less frequent (in narration of *Ahadith*), (and who remained) unknown. (Therefore) a very small number of people reported from him, and that is why such kinds of *Ahadith* remained unknown to the majority of those involved in *fatwa*.

The people of this generation were (fortunate to have) the collections of the *athar* of the Companions and Followers of every city, while people before them could hardly (manage to) collect the *Ahadith* of their own cities and companions. For information on *Asma' al-Rijal* (the biographies of men involved in the narration of *Hadith*) (and for determination of) the degrees of their fairness, people in past used to rely on what they acquired through examination of the conditions and investigation of circumstances. (The *'ulama'* of) this generation, however, closely examined this field and made it a distinct aspect of recording and research.

The (*'ulama'* of this generation) discussed the (question of) giving judgement over the soundness (of *Hadith*) and other aspects of it. As a result they discovered what was hidden of the condition of *ittisal*[62] and *inqita'*. Sufyan, Waki' (b. al-Jarrah d.196AH/811AD) and people like them tried their best, but they could not (manage to collect) more than a thousand *marfū' muttasil Ahadith*[63]. This is according to what Abu Dawud al-Sijistani has mentioned in his *risala* to the people of Makkah.

The people of this generation used to narrate about forty thousand or so *Ahadith*. On the other hand, it has been authentically reported from Bukhari that he condensed his *Sahih* (*al-Bukhari*) out of six thousand *Ahadith*. It is reported on the authority of Abu Dawud that he condensed his *Sunan* out of five thousand *Ahadith*.

(Imam) Ahmad (b. Hanbal) made his *Musnad* a balance (*mīzān*) by which the *Hadith* of the Messenger of Allah (SAAS) could be recognised. So whatever is found therein even through a single line of transmission, would have an origin (*asl*) otherwise it would have no basis.

The leaders of (this generation) were 'Abd al-Rahman b. Mahdi (d.198AH/813AD), Yahya b. Sa'id al-Qattan (d.198AH/813AD), Yazid b. Hārūn (d.206AH/821AD), 'Abd al-Razzaq, Abu Bakr b. Abi Shaiba (d. 235AH/849AD), Musaddad, Hannād, Ahmad b. Hanbal, Ishaq b. Rahawaih (d.238AH/852AD), al-Fadl b. Dukain, 'Ali (b.'Abd Allah b. Ja'far) al-Madini (d.234AH/848AD) and their colleagues.

This was the first class generation of traditionists. After consolidating the field of transmission and the Science of (determining) the degrees of *Ahadith*, the research scholars among the traditionists (of this generation) turned their attention to *Fiqh*. When they found that *Ahadith* and *āthār* were contradicting each of those *madhahib* they decided not to agree on the *taqlid* of someone from the past. So they began investigating *Ahadith* of the Prophet (SAAS) and *athar* of the Companions, Followers and *mujtahidīn* in accordance with the rules they had established themselves, which I will explain to you in simple words.

They were of the opinion that if the Qur'an was clear over an issue, then it was not permissible to turn to something else. And if the Qur'an has the possibility of several meanings then the *Sunnah* would determine its position. And if they did not find (the answer to the question) in the Book of Allah, they would act on the *Sunnah* of the Messenger of Allah (SAAS). (They would act on the *Sunnah*) whether or not it had the widespread circulation among the *Fuqaha'* or whether it was specifically associated with the people of a town or members of a family, or (narrated) through a particular chain, and whether or not the Companions and *Fuqaha'* had acted upon it. If a

Al-Insaf fi bayan sabab al-ikhtilaf

Hadith was available on a particular issue, neither disagreement by any of the *athar* nor *ijtihad* of any *mujtahid* was to be followed.

And if the search for *Ahadith* exhausted them and they did not find a *Hadith* on the issue in question, they would act upon the views of a group of Companions and Followers (And in doing so) they would not restrict themselves exclusively to a particular group of people or a city, as used to be the practice of people before them. If (they found) the majority of Caliphs and *Fuqaha'* agreeing on something then that would be convincing for them. But if they (the Caliphs and *Fuqaha'*) disagreed then they would adhere to the *Hadith* (reported) by the (one who is) most learned, pious, or the one who is more accurate in recording, or the one most renowned among them. If (during this process) they found something for which the two views were equivalent then it would be an issue of two views.

If they were not able to do so, then they would study the general guidelines of the Book (of Allah) and *Sunnah*, their indications and the alluded meanings of their texts. They would apply the precedent of the issue to it for answer if both (the issue and its precedent) were close to each other. (In doing so they would) not rely on the rules of the Principles (of Islamic Jurisprudence) but on what was delivered to the sense and (by which) the heart was satisfied. (This is) just as the balance of *tawātur* (frequency) is neither the number of transmitters (of *Hadith*) nor their conditions, but the certainty that follows in hearts of the people as we have pointed out in our explanation of the conditions of the Companions.

These principles were derived from the work of predecessors and their clear statements. Maymun b. Mihran (d.117AH/735AD) is reported as saying: "It was the practice of Abu Bakr (RA) that when the two parties in a dispute appeared before him he would look into the Book of Allah. If he found therein what decides between them he would pronounce the judgement accordingly. And if it was not available in the Book (of Allah), (but) he knew of a *Sunnah* of the Messenger of Allah (SAAS) on that matter, then he would decide according to it. If (this process) exhausted him he would go out and ask the Muslims: "Such and such (case) has come to me, do you know whether the Messenger of Allah (SAAS) made any judgement in this respect?" (In response) sometimes a whole group of people would turn up and speak of the Messenger of Allah's (SAAS) judgement in that situation. Then Abu Bakr would say: "Praise be to Allah who has made amongst us (such) people who remember (things) from our Prophet (SAAS)". If the search for the *Sunnah* of the Messenger of Allah (SAAS) on that matter exhausted him, he would call a meeting of the chiefs and dignitaries of the community for consultation. If they agreed on something he would decide accordingly".

It is reported on the authority of (Qadi) Shuraih (b. Harith) that 'Umar ibn al-Khattab (RA) wrote to him: "If something about the Book of Allah comes to you, decide according to it, and don't let the people to distract you from it. If what comes to you is not found in the Book of Allah, then look (into) the *Sunnah* of the Messenger of Allah (SAAS) and decide according to it. If what has come to you can not be found in the Book of Allah nor in any *Sunnah* of the Messenger of Allah (SAAS) on that (issue), then look at what the people have agreed upon and act on it. If what has come to you can not be found in the Book of Allah nor in any *Sunnah* of the Messenger of Allah (SAAS), and no one before you has spoken about it, then choose one of the two things: (i) if you wish to apply your own judgement, then go ahead with it, and (ii) if you wish to delay the matter, then delay it, and I don't see delaying but good for you".

It is reported on the authority of 'Abd Allah b. Mas'ud as saying: "There was a time when we did not pronounce the judgement and at that time we were not capable of it. Indeed Allah has determined the matter that we have reached (the situation) that you see, so whosoever from now on is assigned with the (responsibility) of judgment, should decide according to the Book of Allah. If he comes across something not found in the Book of Allah, he should decide in accordance with what the Messenger of Allah (SAAS) has decided. If he comes across something not found in the Book of Allah and no judgement is given by the Messenger of Allah (SAAS), then he should decide in accordance with what the pious people have decided. (And in doing so) he should not say: "I am afraid or this is my opinion". That is because, "What is lawful (*halal*) is evident and what is unlawful (*haram*) is (also) evident, and in between them there are ambiguous matters. So leave that which makes you doubt for that which does not make you doubt".

Whenever ('Abd Allah) b.'Abbas (RA) was asked about something, he would inform of it's (solution) if it was found in the Qur'an, and if it was not found in the Qur'an but was transmitted from the Messenger of Allah (SAAS), he would inform of it. If he did not find it there, then he would (seek its solution) in reports from Abu Bakr and 'Umar (RA). In cases where a solution could not be found there, then he would give his own opinion about it.

It is reported on the authority of Ibn 'Abbas as saying: "Don't you fear to be chastised or swallowed for saying 'the Messenger of Allah (SAAS) said, and so and so said". Qatada (b. Di'amah al-Saddusīd.117AH/735AD) is reported to have said: "(Muhammad) b. Sirin (d.110AH/728AD) related to a man a *Hadith* (reported) from the Prophet (SAAS) and the man said: "So and so said such and such". Ibn Sīrīn said: "I am relating to you the *Hadith* of the Prophet (SAAS) and you are saying, so and so said such and such".

Al-Auza'i is reported to have said: " 'Umar ibn 'Abd al-'Aziz (d.101AH/719AD) wrote: "No one's *ra'i* (arbitrary opinion) has (any standing) as far as the Book of Allah is concerned. Only the opinion of the Imams is (valid) on (a matter) that the Book did not reveal and the *Sunnah* of the Messenger of Allah (SAAS) did not take place. No one's opinion has any validity on a *Sunnah* established by the Messenger of Allah (SAAS)".

(Sulaiman b. Mihran) Al-A'mash (d.148AH/765AD) said: "Ibrahim used to say: "The person following (the imam in prayer) should stand on his (the imam's) left side". But when I related to him the *Hadith* (reported) by Sami' al-Zayyat from Ibn 'Abbas that the Prophet (SAAS) made him stand on his right side, he accepted it". It is reported on the authority of al-Sha'bi that a man came to him and asked him (his opinion) about something. Al-Sha'bi told him: "Ibn Mas'ud used to say so and so", but the man said: "Tell me about your (own) opinion". Al-Sha'bi said: "Are you not surprised at this (man), I informed him of Ibn Mas'ud's (opinion) and he is asking about my opinion. I prefer my religion on that. By Allah! It is dearer to me to sing a song than to let you know of my opinion". All these *āthār* are related by al-Darimi.

Al-Tirmidhi (d. 279AH/892AD) reported Abu'l-Sa'ib as saying: "(Once) we were (sitting) with Waki', who said to a man who held views in favour of *ra'i*: "The Messenger of Allah (SAAS) made a mark on an animal while Abu Hanifa says it is mutilation (*muthla*)". The man said: "It has been reported from Ibrahim al-Nakh'i as saying: "Marking on animal is mutilation". Abu'l-Sa'ib says: "I saw Waki' become very angry and said: "I am telling you what the Messenger of Allah (SAAS) said, and you say: "Ibrahim said (so and so)". Don't you deserve to be detained and not released until you withdraw this statement?"

'Abd Allah b.'Abbas, 'Ata' (b. Abi Rabah), Mujahid (b. Jabr al-Makki d.102AH/720AD) and Malik b. Anas (RA) are reported to have said: "Everyone's statement is open to acceptance or rejection except the saying of the Messenger of Allah (SAAS) (which is always acceptable)".

In short, when they established *Fiqh* on these principles there remained no issue on which their predecessors had spoken or the one which appeared in their own time but they found about it a *Hadith marfū' muttasil* or *mursal* or *mawquf sahih* or *hasan* (good) or the one worth consideration. Or they found about theses things one of the *athar* of *shaikhain* (Abu Bakr and 'Umar RA), or the rest of the Caliphs, judges of big cities and jurists of the country. Or (they found) an inference based on a general guideline, indication or alluded meanings of the text. This is how Allah made practice on *Sunnah* easy for them.

The greatest of them in rank, the most extensive in reporting, the most learned in the degrees of *Hadith* and the most profound among them in *Fiqh* was Ahmad b. Hanbal, then Ishaq b. Rahawaih. The arrangement of *Fiqh* on this pattern depended on collecting a great many *Ahadith* and *athar*. This was so important that Ahmad b.

Al-Insaf fi bayan sabab al-ikhtilaf

Hanbal was asked whether one hundred thousand *Ahadith* would suffice a man to issue *fatwa*? He replied: "No", till it was suggested five hundred thousand *Ahadith*, (to which) he said: "I hope so in the utmost limit". It means that the *fatwa* should be issued according to this principle.

Then Allah created another generation who found that their (predecessor) companions had saved them from the trouble of collecting *Ahadith* and establishing *Fiqh* according to their principles. So they devoted themselves to other fields. (One of them was) to select those sound *Ahadith* on which there has been consensus among the major traditionists such as Yazid[64] b. Harun, Yahya b. Sa'id al-Qattan, Ahmad (b. Hanbal), Ishaq (b. Rahawaih) and the likes. (And secondly to) collect those *Ahadith* of *Fiqh* upon which the *Fuqaha'* of big cities and *'ulama'* of the country based their *madhahib*. Or (thirdly) to pass judgement on every *Hadith* what it deserves, and the *Ahadith* like *shādha*[65] and *fādha* (unique), which they did not relate. Or (fourthly to give ruling on) chains (of such *Ahadith*) from which the predecessors did not deduce (and) which contained *ittisal* or *uluwwu sanad*[66]. (Similarly they focussed on judging) the report of a *Faqih* from another *Faqih*, or a *hāfiz* (of *Hadith*) from another *hāfiz* and (other) academic issues of this kind.

These (traditionists) are Bukhari, Muslim, Abu Dawūd, 'Abd b. Humaid, Al-Darimi, Ibn Majah (d. 273AH/886AD), Abu Ya'la (d. 276AH/889AD), Al-Tirmidhi, al-Nasa'ī, Al-Daraqutni (d.385AH/996AD), Al-Hakīm (d. 405AH/1014AD), Al-Baihaqi (d. 458AH/1065AD), Al-Khatīb (Al-Baghdadi d. 403AH/1012AD), Al-Daylami, Ibn 'Abd al-Barr (d. 463AH/1070AD) and (others) like them.

In my view the most comprehensive of them in knowledge, the most useful in writing and the most renowned among them, are four men of approximately (similar) period. The first of them is Abu 'Abd Allah al-Bukhari. His purpose was to select the *mustafida*[67] sound *muttasil Ahadith* from the rest and then to deduce from them *Fiqh*, *Sirah* and *Tafsir*. Consequently he composed his *Jāmi' al-Sahih* and accomplished what he had stipulated. We have been told that a pious man saw the Messenger of Allah (SAAS) in his dream saying: "Why have you preoccupied yourself with the *Fiqh* of Muhammad b. Idris (Shafi'i) and abandoned my book?" He said: "O Messenger of Allah! What is your book?" He replied: "*Sahih al-Bukhari*". By my life! Bukhari gained such a (high) degree of reputation and popularity beyond which nothing more is desired.

The second among them is Muslim al-Nishapuri (d. 261AH/874AD). His aim was to revive those sound *Ahadith* upon which there has been agreement among the traditionists (and which are) *muttasil marfu'*, and from which the *Sunnah* is inferred. He wanted to bring them closer to minds and to facilitate inference from them. He produced an excellent arrangement and gathered *turuq* of every *Hadith* in one place so that the difference of texts (of *Hadith*) becomes clear and the ramification of chains clearer as much as possible. He reconciled between those *Ahadith* which were different in text but were of similar meanings (*al-mukhtalifat*) and (thus) left no excuse for any one conversant with Arabic language to turn away from *Sunnah* to something else.

The third of them is Abu Dawud al-Sijistani. His main concern was to collect those *Ahadith* from which the *Fuqaha'* inferred and which remained in circulation among them, and upon which the *'ulama'* of big cities founded laws. So he composed his *Sunan* and assembled therein the sound (*al-sihah*), good (*hasan*), easy (*al-layyin*)[68] and *Ahadith* worth practising (*salih lil 'amal*). Abu Dawud says: "I did not mention in my book any *Hadith* that the people agreed should be abandoned. He clearly stated weakness of a weak *Hadith*, and the one which had an *ailment* (*'illa*), he explained it in such a way that it could (easily) be recognised by the one concerned with this matter. He wrote biographies of everyone who narrated *Hadith* from which a scholar inferred and a follower of (*madhhab*) adopted (his view). This is why al-Ghazali (Abu Hamid d.505AH/1111AD) and others declared that his book is sufficient for *mujtahid*.

The fourth of them is Abu 'Isa al-Tirmidhi (d.279AH/892AD). It would appear that he improved the method of *shaikhain* (Bukhari and

Muslim) as they explained (well) and left no ambiguity. (Similarly he improved) the method of Abu Dawud (whose aim) was to collect all that (which) has been adhered to by an adherent. As a result al-Tirmidhi combined both these methods in addition to explaining the *madhahib* of Companions, Followers and *Fuqaha'* of big cities. So he compiled a comprehensive book and condensed the *turuq* of *Hadith*. He mentioned one and pointed out to others. He explained the position of every *Hadith* whether it was sound, good, *da'if* (weak) or *munkar*[69]. He explained the reason of weakness (in *Hadith*) so that the student of *Hadith* (*talib*) may have the insight of his endeavour, and recognised that which was suitable for consideration than others. He mentioned whether the *Hadith* was *mustafid* or *gharib* as well as explaining the views of the Companions and *Fuqaha'* of big cities. He named the person who needed naming and gave surname to the person who needed surname and left no secrecy about any man of knowledge. It is therefore said that this (book) is sufficient for *mujtahid* and will make a *muqallid* independent (of other books).

In comparison to these (people mentioned above) there were (other) people during the period of Malik and Sufyan and after them who did not dislike (discussing) the *masa'il*, and were not afraid of (giving) *fatwa*. They maintained that the foundation of religion depends on *Fiqh*; therefore its propagation was necessary. However, they were afraid of reporting the *Hadith* of the Messenger of Allah (SAAS) and ascribing it to him. (They were so serious in this attitude) that al-Sha'bi said: "(To ascribe the *Hadith*) to someone other one the Prophet (SAAS) is dearer to us, because if there is any addition or deficiency therein (the burden of responsibility) would lie on someone other than the Prophet (SAAS)". Ibrahim used to say: "I (prefer to) say, 'Abd Allah said and 'Alqama said. (This) is dearer to us (than to ascribe the *Hadith* to the Prophet (SAAS)".

When Ibn Mas'ud used to narrate the *Hadith* from the Messenger of Allah (SAAS), his face would become ashen, and he would say: "This way or like that".

When 'Umar (RA) sent a group of Ansar to Kufa, he told them: "You are going to Kufa and there you will meet a people who wail over the Qur'an. They will come to you and say: "The Companions of Muhammad (SAAS) have arrived, the Companions of Muhammad (SAAS) have arrived". They would come to you to ask you about the *Hadith,* so lessen the reporting (of *Ahadith*) from the Messenger of Allah (SAAS)".

Ibn 'Awn says: "When something appeared to al-Sha'bi, he would observe precaution, while Ibrahim would keep on talking". These *āthār* are related by al-Darimi.

The recording of *Hadith, Fiqh* and *masa'il* became their concern from another aspect (as well). That is because they did not have that much *Ahadith* and *āthār* (which could have) enabled them to infer *Fiqh* in accordance with the principles adopted by the traditionists. Nor were their hearts opened to the examination, collection and investigation of the views of scholars of the (whole) country. For this they blamed themselves.

They held their leaders in the highest degree of academic inquiry and their hearts were more inclined towards their companions. This is just as 'Alqama said: "Is any one among them (Companions) more reliable (in *Fiqh*) than 'Abd Allah (b. Mas'ud)?" Abu Hanifa said: "Ibrahim is more knowledgeable (in *Fiqh*) than Salim, and if it were not for the superiority of Companionship, I would have said that 'Alqama is more knowledgeable than ('Abd Allah) b.'Umar".

They were endowed with intelligence, intuition and swift movement of mind from one thing to another, which enabled them to deduce the answers of *masa'il* according to the teachings of their companions. (This is just as they say) "Everything is made convenient for what it has been created", (and the Qur'anic verse) "Each party rejoices in what it has got."[70]

(This is how) they established *Fiqh* on the principle of *takhrij* (deduction). This means that every one should preserve the book of the spokesman of his companions who is most conversant with the teachings of the group and has most sound insight in preference (*tarjih*)[71]. This is because with regard to each *mas'ala* he may seriously think over the purpose of the law. So whenever he is asked about something or he feels the need to (know) about something he could look into what he has preserved of his companions' statements. If he finds the answer (therein) it would be all right, otherwise he would look at the generalities of their statement and would apply it on this pattern. Or (he would look at) a supplementary reference in their statement and infer from it accordingly.

Sometimes the statement (of a scholar) may contain indication or alluded meaning, which helped in understanding the purpose (of that statement). Sometimes the question being explained may have a precedent, which could be construed in that sense. Sometimes they used to examine the cause of the law being explained by deduction or by easiness and omission (*al-yusr wa 'l-hadhf*), and applied its rule to the one not being explained. Sometimes there were two statements (of a scholar) which if combined together on the pattern of Conjugate or Conditional Syllogism (*al-Qiyas al-Iqtirani aw al-Shartī*)[72]; both would produce answer of the question. Sometimes their statement may contain what (could be) known by example (*mithāl*), and comparison and contrast (*al-qisma*) (and which could) not (be) known by comprehensively exclusive definition (*al-hadd al-jāmi' al-māni'*).

In such circumstances they would turn to the linguists, and resort to mannerism in order to get to the essential elements (of that statement). And (also) to arrange an exclusively comprehensive definition for it, and to define precisely its obscurity and differentiate its difficult aspects. Sometimes their statements may have the possibility of containing two views (in which case) they would consider giving preference (*tarjīh*) to either of the two probabilities. Sometimes to bring closer (varying) arguments over the issues would be unclear and so they would make clarification. Sometimes those involved in the deduction would infer from the action, silence and (other) similar things of their leaders.

So this is (all) what is (called) deduction (*takhrīj*). They used to say 'this is the deduced view of so and so, and according to the *madhhab* of so and so or according to the principle of so and so, or according to the statement of so and so the answer to the question is such and such. All those (involved in deduction) are called '*al-*

mujtahidūn fi'l-madhhab. This (type of) *ijtihad* according to this principle is meant by those who maintain that whoever memorised *kitab al-Mabsūt* is a *mujtahid*. It means (he will be regarded *mujtahid*) even if he has no knowledge of reporting at all, and knows no single *Hadith*.

So (this is how) *takhrīj* took place in every *madhhab* and (this is how it) developed. Whichever *madhhab*'s followers were well known, they were entrusted with (the position of) judgement and *ifta*. Their writings became popular among the masses and they openly taught (their books and views). (This is why that *madhhab*) spread out in (various) parts of the earth, and is still spreading. Any *madhhab* whose followers were less known, they did not assume the (offices) of judgment and *ifta'*, and did not win over the interest of the people, (such a *madhhab*) became extinct after a while.

Fiqh between the two extremes

Behold that *takhrīj* is based on (deduction of an issue) from the statement of *Fuqaha'* and the study of the text of *Hadith*. Both of these (foundations) have deep-rooted origins in religion and in every age the research scholars have been acting on both of them. Some of them are less frequent with (*takhrij*) and more frequent with (the study of *Hadith*), (while) others are more frequent with this and advocate it, (but) are less frequent with that. Therefore the position of either of the two should not be completely overlooked just as the majority of the two groups do. On the contrary the sheer fairness (demands) that each should be conformed to other and the deficiency of one should be supplemented with other.

And this has been the view of Hasan al-Basri. (He said:) "By Allah except whom there is no god, your *Sunnah* is in between these two (extremes), between the excess and deficiency (*al-ghālī wa'l-jafī*). So whoever belongs to *Ahl al-Hadith* should present what he has adopted and adheres to the *ra'i* of *mujtahidin* among the Followers and those after them. And the one who belongs to *Ahl al-takhrīj* should study *Sunan* in order to avoid as far as possible violation of clear and sound (*Hadith*) and from giving his personal opinion on matters where a *Hadith* or *athar* is available".

(Similarly) for a traditionist it is not appropriate to probe into the rules firmly established by his companions and (which) have been not specified by the *Law Giver*. (Because in doing so) he may reject a *Hadith* or a sound analogy such as the rejection of that in which there is a minute suspicion of *irsal* and *inqita'*. (This will be) just like Ibn Hazm (d. 456AH/1064AD) did. He rejected *Hadith Tahrīm al-ma'āzif* (prohibition of stringed instruments) because of the suspicion of *inqita'* in the report of Bukhari. The *Hadith* itself, however, is *muttasil sahih* because this kind of (situation) happens only when there is contradiction.

Similarly when they say that 'so and so remembers more *Ahadith* than others and for this reason they prefer the *Hadith* (reported by him) than to (the one reported by) the other even though the other one had thousand reasons of *tarjih* (preference).

While reporting the *Hadith* with meaning (*al-riwaya bi'l-ma'na*), the majority of transmitters were concerned with the main meanings and not those considerations which are familiar to the specialists of Arabic. Their argumentation was over (things) like *fa'* and *waw'*, and putting a word forward or backward and other kinds of in depth probing. (This is) because often (when) the other narrator mentions that story he replaces that letter with another letter.

In fact whatever the transmitter comes up with, it is obvious that it is the statement of the Prophet (SAAS). So if there appears another *Hadith* or another evidence it becomes necessary to turn to it. It is not appropriate for the one involved in deduction to deduce a statement not supported by the statement of his companions, and which is not comprehensible to those conversant with the customs and the linguists, and (therefore that statement) would be conditional upon *takhrij*.

Interpretation of a precedent of a case in its sense is one of those (issues) over which there has been disagreement and clash of opinion among the prominent '*ulama'*. If his companions are asked about that *mas'ala*, they may not construe the precedent in the sense of precedent. This is because of an objection (in their view) or they may mention an '*illa* other than that deduced by him.

On the contrary *takhrij* is allowed because it actually pertains to the *taqlid* of *mujtahid* and is not accomplished but in the context of what is understood of his statement. Similarly (the one involved in deduction) should not reject a *Hadith* or an *athar* upon which the people have agreed. (He should not do so) on the basis of a principle deduced by him and his companions. Take for example the rejection of *Hadith al-Musarrāt*[73] and (the *Hadith* concerning) the annulment of the shares of relatives.

This is because consideration for *Hadith* is more necessary than consideration for that deduced rule. To this (very) fact Shafi'i pointed out in his statement: "Whatever view or principle I make, if (something) from the Messenger of Allah (SAAS) appears contrary to what I said, the (final) word is then that said by him (SAAS)".

In the beginning of his book "*Ma'ālim al-Sunan*" Imam Abu Sulaiman (Hamd b. Muhammad) al-Khattabi (d.388AH/999AD) has very skilfully cited the instances (of this phenomenon). He says: "I find men of knowledge in our time have become two parties and divided into two groups-the supporters of *Hadith* and tradition and the proponents of *Fiqh* and opinion (*nazar*). Neither of them distinguishes (itself) from its counterpart in (its) need, nor does it dispense with it in accomplishing the same kind of purpose and aim. This is because the *Hadith* is like a foundation, which is the origin, while *Fiqh* is like a building, which in relation to (*Hadith*) is like a branch. And any building, which is not laid down on foundation is (bound) to collapse, and any foundation void of building and structure is a desert and ruin.

In view of the closeness of their locations and destinations, general dependency on each other and complete indispensability with each other I found these two groups as brothers. But despite this they part from each other on the path of truth and do not support and co-operate with each other.

As for this group who are the advocates of *Hadith* and *athar*, most of them seem concerned with reports, collection of chains, and search for *gharib* and *shadh Hadith*, most of which are fabricated or changed (*maqlub*)[74]. They do not care for the texts and do not try to understand their meanings. Neither do they find out the secrets nor do they extract their precious contents and *Fiqh*. Mostly they find faults in *Fuqaha'*, vilify them and accuse them of violating the *Sunan*. They do not realise the fact that they (themselves) are incapable of attaining the degree of knowledge bestowed upon those people, and (thus they) commit sin by speaking ill of them.

As for the other group who are *Ahl al-Fiqh wa'l-nazar*, most of them rarely turn to *Hadith* and can hardly distinguish between sound and unsound (*Ahadith*). Neither do they differentiate between the perfect and faulty (*Ahadith*). They do not care about what has reached them of the *Hadith* to advance it as an argument against their adversaries when it conforms to their *madhahib* to which they adhere and (which) agrees to the opinions they subscribe to.

They (*Ahl al-Fiqh*) have agreed among themselves on accepting the weak *Hadith*. If *Hadith al-munqati'* had become well known in their view and had gained widespread circulation among themselves, (they would accept it) without having authenticity or certainty of knowledge over it. This (attitude) would be (considered) an error of judgement and fault on their part.

May Allah bless them and us with success, if a statement by one of the chiefs of their *madhab* and leaders of their inclination is related to them, which speaks of his *ijtihad*, they would ask for confidence in him and seek his exoneration from charge. You will find that the companions of Malik in respect of his *madhhab* rely on nothing but only on what is related from Ibn al-Qasim, al-Ashhab and others like them among his noble companions. If a report from 'Abd Allah b.'Abd al-Hakim and his likes is mentioned it is of no use in their view.

(Similarly) you will notice the companions of Abu Hanifa do not accept a report from him but only that which is narrated by Abu Yusuf, Muhammad b. al-Hasan, his prominent companions and great students. (But) if a report contrary to his view comes to them from Hasan b. Ziyad al-Lu'lu'i (d. 204AH/819-20AD) and someone below his rank, they would not accept and rely on it. Likewise you will find the companions of Shafi'i discussing his *madhhab* only according to the report of al-Muzani and al-Rabi'a b. Sulayman al-Muradi. If the report of Harmala, Buhtari and others like them is mentioned they do not take it into consideration and do not rely upon its teachings.

This has been the attitude of *'ulama'* of each group regarding the laws of the *madhahib* of their imams and teachers. So if this was their practice, and while they were not content with regard to these *furū'* and reporting them from those *shuyukh* but through authentication and verification, then how could it be permissible for them to be careless in respect of the most important matter and the greatest concern. And (how can they) be indifferent with regard to the reporting and transmission from the Imam of the Imams and the Messenger of the Lord of Honour, whose order is obligatory, obedience binding and to whose authority submission and obedience compulsory for us inasmuch as that we do not find in ourselves any objection to what he has decreed, and no rancour in our hearts against what he has (firmly) established and executed.

What do you think of a man who is less careful in his own affairs, treats his debtors with kindness, accepts counterfeit from them and passes judgement of no fault in their favour? Would he be allowed to do the same with regard to someone on whose behalf he is acting, such as guardian of the weak, trustee of the orphan and attorney of the absentee? If he does so, will it not be on his part a betrayal of trust and breach of obligation? So this is what it is, either it could be perceived through immediate sensual experience or through comparison (and analogy).

But it could be that some people might have experienced the path of truth hard and found the time for achieving the fortune longer. They wished to have quick gain, and therefore they shortened the path of learning. They contented themselves with bits and pieces, and letters drawn from the meanings of the Principles of Jurisprudence, which they called '*ilal*. They made these (bits and pieces) as their mottos by portraying the forms of knowledge and used them like shields to encounter the adversaries. They set them as targets for disputation and polemic, on which they argued and clashed with each other. At the conclusion (of their debates) the verdict of intelligence and superiority is accorded to the victor. So (from now on) he would be the celebrated jurist of his time and the august leader of his country and city.

What's more, the devil has intrigued against them (another) subtle trick. He worked on them a profound plot by suggesting to them: "What you know is a little knowledge and an insignificant commodity, which cannot satisfy the extent of (your) need and (fulfil) sufficiency. (You may) conquer it with scholastic theology and supplement it with its bits and pieces. (Moreover), seek help through the principles of theologians (because) it widens man's field of discussion and scope of examination". Thus the devil proved true his idea on them and a great many of them followed and obeyed him except a group of (sincere) believers. What a shame on men and their intelligence! Which way is their intelligence leading them and how is the devil deceiving them of their fortune and their (true) place of guidance? Allah is the one whose help is (to be) sought". (Here) ends the statement of al-Khattabi.

Conditions of *Fiqh* before the 4th century

Reasons for differences between the predecessors and successors over affiliation and non-affiliation to a *madhhab*

Behold that people in the first and second centuries did not agree on *taqlid* (imitation) of a particular *madhhab*. Abu Talib al-Makki states in (Kitab) *Qūt al-Qulūb*: "The books and collections are innovations, (likewise) advocating the views of (particular) people. (Similarly) giving *fatwa* according to the *madhhab* of a particular person, adhering to his view, relating to him in every thing, and relying on his *madhhab* (are later inventions). The people practised (none of such things) in the past first and second centuries". (Here) ends (the statement of Abu Talib al-Makki).

Rather there were two types of people: the *'ulama'* and the masses. As for the masses, it was admirable of them that on those collective matters on which there was no disagreement among the Muslims or among the majority of *mujtahidīn*, they used to imitate only the *Law Giver* (SAAS). They used to learn the method of *wudū, ghusl*, rules of *salah* and *zakah* and (other such) things from their forefathers or teachers of their towns. This was their common practice. And if there appeared something unusual they would seek *fatwa* from any *mufti* they could find without specification of *madhhab*.

At the end of (his book) *al-Tahrīr* Ibn al-Humām (d. 861AH/1457AD) states that sometimes peope used to consult one *mufti* and sometimes others without committing themselves to a (particular) *mufti*. Here (ends the statement).

As for *'ulama'*, they were of two categories. Some of them devoted themselves to the study of the Book (of Allah), *Sunnah* and *athar* to such an extent that they acquired actual ability (of understanding the *Shari'a*) to be appointed as *muftis* for the people. (As *muftis*) they were able to answer the queries of the people which were mostly about day to day events. The answers of questions given by them were more than those on which they deferred their judgement. (A scholar of this category) was given the title of *al-mujtahid al-mutlaq*.

Sometimes this ability was achievable through strenuous efforts in the collection of reports. This is because most of the laws have been mentioned in *Ahadith, āthār* of Companions, Followers and the Followers of Followers. (In addition, it was also important to be equipped) with what an intelligent person (who is) conversant with (Arabic) language cannot remain detached from learning about the contexts of speech. (Likewise) the one familiar with *āthār* (cannot remain detached) from learning the methods of *al-jam' bayn al-mukhtalifat* (reconciliation between inconsistent or contradictory *Ahadith*), and the arrangement of arguments and other issues of this kind. Such is the case of the two ideal Imams Ahmad b. Muhammad b. Hanbal and Ishaq b. Rahawaih.

And sometimes this ability was attainable through consolidating the methods of *takhrij* and accurately recording the principles reported from the *masha'ikh* of *Fiqh* in every field. (These principles) belonged to the rules and regulations (of *takhrij*). (In addition, he would have the knowledge of) all the sound *Sunan* and *athar*. Such is the case of the two ideal Imams Abu Yusuf and Muhammad b. al-Hasan.

(The second category of *'ulama'*) were those who acquired so much knowledge of Qur'an and *Sunan* that it enabled them to have (all) the information about the transmitters of *Fiqh* and its main cases through their detailed evidences. They were (also) able to make strong opinion about some other (minor) cases through their evidences. However, there were some other cases over which they deferred their judgement. For such cases they needed consultation with (senior) *'ulama'* because they had not (yet) gained the command in the means possessed by *mujtahid al-mutlaq*. Such (a jurist) would be (regarded) *mujtahid* in some matters and *non-mujtahid* in others.

It has been frequently reported of the Companions and Followers that whenever a *Hadith* reached them they acted upon it without attaching any condition to it. It was after the (first) two centuries that people began adhering to the *madhhab* of a particular *mujtahid* and those who did not rely on the *madhhab* of a particular *mujtahid* were very few.

This was the order of the day. This is because the one involved in *Fiqh* is not free from two conditions. Firstly, his main concern should be to know those cases, which have been answered by previous *mujtahidin* through their detailed evidences. (Those evidences) and their sources were subjected to (rigorous) criticism and scrutiny, and then some of them were given preference over others (by those *mujtahidin*).

This is a big task, which can only be accomplished by following an imam who had taken considerable trouble of explaining the cases and furnishing evidences in every field. Thus he would (be able to) benefit from him. After accomplishing this he should engage in criticism and *tarjīh* (of the views and evidences). If this imam was not available it would have been difficult for him (to have acquired this information), and there is no sense in pursuing a difficult matter while there is possibility of an easy one.

It is necessary for this follower (*muqtadī*) to be good at what his imam has preceded him and supplement him with something (deficient) of him. If his supplementation is less than his agreement (with his imam) he is reckoned among the prominent members of the *madhhab,* and if it is more, then his uniqueness is not regarded as significant in the *madhhab*. However, on the whole he remains affiliated to the founder of his *madhhab* and will be distinguished from the one who follows another imam in many *usul* and *furu'* of his *madhhab*. Jurists like him would have produced some results of their efforts of *ijtihad* in finding answers of questions not answered before. This is because events have been happening frequently and the door (of *ijtihad* has remained) open. So (a jurist like him) deduces (answers based on his own *ijtihad*) from the Book (of Allah), *Sunnah* and *athar* of predecessors without relying on his imam. But (such answers) would be few in comparison to those answered before. And (a jurist like) this is called *al-mujtahid al-mutlaq al-muntasib*.

The second (of the conditions mentioned above) is that his

(*Faqih*'s) main concern should be to learn about those cases, which the questioners ask about and which have not been dealt with by the predecessors. His need to follow an imam in the principles established in every field (of *Fiqh*) is greater than that of the first one (discussed above). This is because the *masa'il* of *Fiqh* are interlinked and interwoven, and its *furu'* are connected with their *usul*.

So if he begins with the criticism of (predecessors') *madhahib* and scrutinises their views he would be committing himself to something which he is unable to do. He would not be able to finish it off throughout his life. Therefore he has no other way in respect of what concerns him but to examine what has been done before and devote his attention to sub-divisions (*al-tafarī'*). Jurists like him may have supplemented their imams on the basis of the Book (of Allah), *Sunnah, athar* of predecessors and analogy but these are few in comparison to their concordances. And (a jurist like) this is called *al-mujtahid fi'l-madhhab*.

As for the third condition, it means that at first he should devote his efforts to learn those evidences, which have been made before him. Then he should devote again his efforts at ramification of what he has selected and excelled at. This is due to the fact that this is a far-off unreal situation because of the distance of period from the time of revelation, and (because) most of that which is necessary for every scholar to be conversant with, depends on people of the past.

These (needs) relate to the transmission of *Ahadith* according to the ramification of their texts and chains (of authorities), knowledge of the ranks of transmitters, and the degrees of soundness of *Hadith* and its weakness. (He also needs to) collect those *Ahadith* and *āthār* in which there are differences and to be aware of the sources of *Fiqh* therein. (He should also be) familiar with the obscurity of language and Principles of *Fiqh*, transmission of those *masa'il* which have been discussed by the predecessors in spite of their great number, disparity and diversity. (Then he should) concentrate his thoughts on differentiation of those reports and subject them to evidences.

If he spends (all) his life in (fulfilling those needs, then) how can he do justice to *tafarī'* (derivatives) after that, because human soul even if it is honest, has certain limitations beyond which it cannot go. This (exceptional ability) was available only to first-class *mujtahidin* when the period (of the Prophet SAAS) was near and the sciences were not divided. Even then this was possible for only few people. Despite that they followed their *masha'ikh* and relied upon them, but because of the multitude of their dispositions in knowledge they became independent.

In general adherence to the *madhhab* of *mujtahidin* is a secret Allah al-Mighty inspired *'ulama'* with and united them upon it whether they realise it or not. Among the instances we have mentioned is the statement of *Faqih* Ibn Ziyad al-Shafi'i al-Yamani mentioned in his *fatawa*. Accordingly, he was asked about the two cases which were answered by al-Bulqini contrary to the *madhhab* of Shafi'i. (In response the former) said: "You do not understand the interpretation of the statement of al-Bulqini unless you know his position in knowledge (of *Fiqh*). This is because he is *imam mujtahid mutlaq muntasib ghair mustaqil* and he is capable of conducting *takhrij* and *tarjih*[75]. By *mutlaq al-muntasib* I mean the one who applies *ikhtiar*[76] and *tarjih* against the preferred view of the *madhhab* of the imam to whom he is affiliated". This is the position of many great and senior companions of Shafi' among the previous and later scholars who will be mentioned shortly together with order of their ranks.

Among those (*Fuqaha'*) arranged by al-Bulqini in the string of *mujtahidin al-mutlaqin al-muntasibin* is his student Abu Zar'a. He says: "Once I asked our shaikh Imam al-Bulqini: "What makes Shaikh Taqi al-Din al-Subki incapable of *ijtihad* while he has gained perfection in its means, and so why (then) he practises *taqlid*?" Abu Zar'a says: "I did not mention him, i.e. my shaikh al-Bulqini out of respect, because I wanted to draw conclusion (on the basis of his answer)". He became quiet. Then I said: "I think what prevents (*Fuqaha'*) from (practising) (*ijtihad*) is nothing but those assignments which are allocated to the jurists of the four schools of *Fiqh*. So anyone who steps out of that (arrangement) and exercises *ijtihad* would not get anything out of that and will be deprived from the office of judgement. People will avoid consulting him for *fatwa* and he will be charged with innovation. In response he (al-Bulqini) smiled and approved my views on that matter". Here (ends the statement).

I say as far as I am concerned I don't think this may be the case. Allah forbid that their high status prevents them from (*ijtihad*), and that despite being capable of it they could abandon it for the sake of judgement and (other) reasons. No one has the right to assume (such notion) about them. It has been stated earlier that the preferred opinion in view of the majority (of *Fuqah'*) is that (application of) *ijtihad* (becomes) necessary in such kinds (of circumstances). Then how far Wali Abu Zar'a is justified in ascribing that (notion) to them and its approval to Bulqini.

(On this subject) there is a statement of (Imam) Jalal al-Din al-Suyuti in his commentary on *al-Tanbīh*. During discussion on the chapter of divorce he said: "Whatever disagreement happened among the imams because of the alteration in *ijtihad* they used to rectify in every place what led to their *ijtihad* at that time. The author of *al-Tanbih* occupied an undeniable position in *ijtihad*. It has been confirmed by more than one imam that he (author of *al-Tanbīh*), Ibn al Sabbagh, Imam al-Haramayn and al-Ghazali attained the degree of *al-ijtihad al-mutlaq*. And what has been mentioned by Ibn al-Salah (Abu 'Umar 'Uthman d. 643AH/1245AD) in his *fatawa* that they attained the degree of *ijtihad fi'l-madhhab* and not *al-mutlaq*, means that their degree of *ijtihad* was *al-muntasib*, and not *al-mustaqil*".

(*Al-ijtihad*) *al-mutlaq* as confirmed by him (Ibn al-Salah) in his book *Ādāb al-Futya* and by al-Nawawi (d.676AH/1277AD) in '*Sharh al-Muhadhdhab*' is of two kinds: (1) *Al-mustaqil*, which has been extinct since the beginning of the fourth century and since then its existence, has not been possible. (2) *Al-Muntasib*, which will remain (effective) until the major signs of the *Hour* appear. From the *Shari'a* point of view its discontinuation is not allowed because it is a collective duty (*fard kifaya*) and when people of a time fail to fulfil (this duty) and eventually abandon it they would all become sinful and disobedient. This has been made clear by the companions (of Shafi') including al-Mawardi in *al-Hawi,* al-Ruwayyani in *al-Bahr,* and al-Baghawi ('Abd Allah b. Muhammad d.317AH/829AD) in *al-Tahdhib* and others. This duty cannot be discharged through restricted *ijtihad* (*al-muqayyad*). This (view) has been clearly stated by Ibn al-Salah and al-Nawawi in *Sharh al-Muhadhdhab*. The issue has (also) been explained in detail in our book, entitled:

الرد الى من أخلد الى الارض و جهل أنّ الاجتهاد فى كلّ عصر فرض

Those (*Fuqaha'* mentioned above) are not excluded from *ijtihad al-mutlaq al-muntasib* for being Shafi'ites just as has been made clear by al-Nawawi and Ibn al-Salah in *al-Tabaqāt* and followed by Ibn al-Subki. That is why they wrote books on (their) *madhhab*, gave *fatwa* and held Shafi'ite positions. For example the author (of *al-Tanbih*) and Ibn al-Sabbagh held teaching (position) at al-Nizamiya (school) of Baghdad and Imam al-Haramayn and al-Ghazali held teaching positions in Nizamiya at Nishapur. (Likewise) Ibn 'Abd al-Salam (taught) in al-Jabiya and al-Zahiriya at Cairo, and Ibn Daqiq al-'Id in al-Salahiya, in the vicinity of the mausoleum of our Imam Shafi'i, at al-Fadiliya and al-Kamiliya, and other (places).

As for the one who attained the degree of *ijtihad al-mustaqil*, this excludes him from being Shafi'i and his views are not reported in the books of the *madhhab*. I don't know anyone among the companions (of Shafi'i) who attained this position except Abu Ja'far ibn Jarir al-Tabari (d. 224AH/310AD). He was indeed a Shafi'i, then he became independent of *madhhab*, and that is why al-Rafi'i and others said that his uniqueness is not considered significant in *madhhab*". Here (ends the statement).

This in my view is better than what Wali Abu Zar'a has done except that his statement means that Ibn Jarir is not considered a Shafi'i and that is rejected. In the beginning of *kitab al-Zakah* of *al-Sharh* (*al-Wajiz* of al-Ghazali), al-Rafi'i ('Abd al-Karim b. Muhammad al-Qazwini (d. 623AH/1226AD) said: "Ibn Jarir's unique position is not considered significant in our *madhhab* even though he is reckoned among *Tabaqat al-Shafi'iya*". Al-Nawawi states in *al-Tahdhib* that Abu 'Asim al-'Ibadi mentioned him among the Shaf'i *Fuqaha'* and said: "He is one of our unique scholars, he studied *Fiqh* of Shafi'i under Rabi'a al-Muradi and Hasan al-Za'farani". His affiliation to Shafi'i means that he followed his (Shafi'i's) method in *ijtihad*, thorough investigation of evidences and arrangement of some of them over others according to his *ijtihad*. He opposed him on some occasions (but) did not care about (this) opposition. (Despite that) he did not deviate from the method (of Shafi'i) except in some cases, and that does not depreciate his inclusion in the *madhhab* of Shafi'i. And same is the case of Muhammad b. Isma'il al-Bukhari, because he is reckoned among *Tabaqat al-Shafi'iya*. Among those who have mentioned him among *Tabaqat al-Shafi'ya* is Shaikh Taj al-Din al-Subki. He said: "He (Bukhari) studied *Fiqh* under al-Humaydi and al-Humaydi studied it under Shafi'i". Our learned Shaikh furnished evidence for the inclusion of Bukhari among the Shafi'ites by mentioning him in their *Tabaqat*, and the statement of al-Nawawi we have mentioned is an evidence in his support".

In his *Tabaqat (al-Shafi'iyya al-Kubrā)* Shaikh Taj al-Din al-Subki states: "Every *takhrij* applied by the one involved in the deduction has to be examined whether he has been influenced by the *madhhab* and *taqlid* like Abu Hamid and Qifal. (If this is the case then his *takhrij*) would be considered as part of (his) *madhhab*. And if he is one of those whose disagreement (with his own *madhhab*) is frequent like the four Muhammads i.e. Muhammad b. Jarir, Muhammad b. Khuzaima, Muhammad b. Nasr al-Marwazi and Muhammad b. al-Mundhir, then (it) will not be recognised. As for al-Muzani and after him Ibn Suraij, they are between the two categories (of *mujtahidin*). They did not apply disagreement like that of Muhammads nor did they observe restriction (*taqyīd*) like the *taqyid* of 'Iraqis and Khurasanians". (Here) ends (the statement).

Al-Subki in his *Tabaqāt* has mentioned Shaikh Abu'l-Hasan al-Ash'ari the Imam of *Ahl-al-Sunnah wa'l-Jama'ah* saying that he is reckoned among Shafi'is because he studied *Fiqh* under Shaikh Abu Ishaq al-Marwazi. (Here) ends the statement of Ibn Ziyad.

Among the instances we have mentioned is also what (has appeared) in *kitab al-Anwār* where the (author) says: "Those affiliated to the *madhhab* of Shafi'i, Abu Hanifa, Malik or Ahmad b. Hanbal are (of different) kinds. One of them is the common people whose *taqlid* to Shafi'i emanates from the *taqlid* of the one affiliated (to the former).

Secondly, those who have attained the degree of *ijtihad*. A *mujtahid* does not imitate a *mujtahid*, on the contrary they are referred to him because of their adherence to his method in *ijtihad*, application of evidences and arrangement of some of them over others.

Thirdly, those of the middle ranks. These are those who had not attained the degree of *ijtihad*, but have become acquainted with the principles of their imam and became capable of (applying) analogy to what they did not find determined by him. They are *muqallidūn* (imitators) to him and similarly the common people who adhere to their view. However, it is generally believed that they (the former) themselves do not observe *taqlid* because they are *muqalladūn* (the ones whose *taqlid* is observed by others)." Here ends the statement of *kitab al-Anwār*.

If you say how can one thing be non-obligatory in one time and obligatory in another time despite (the fact that) *Sharī'a* is the same, (so on this basis) your statement that adherence to *mujtahid mustaqil* was (previously) not obligatory (and) then it became obligatory is a contradictory and incompatible statement. (In reply) I say: "What is actually obligatory is that in *ummah* there should be someone who knows secondary laws (*al-ahkām al-far'īyya*) through their detailed evidences. On this issue there has been consensus among the righteous people and to give precedence to an obligation is (itself) obligatory. So if there are various ways of (acting on) *wajib*, action on one of them without specification becomes necessary, and if one way is determined for him then that particular way becomes necessary for him.

This is just as if a man was extremely hungry and feared death. If there were several means of eliminating starvation (such as) buying food, picking up fruits from the desert and hunting down something that will provide nourishment, (then) getting any of these means

Al-Insaf fi bayan sabab al-ikhtilaf

without specification becomes necessary. If he arrives in a place where there is neither the (possibility of) hunting nor fruit, (then) it is necessary for him to spend money to buy food.

Similarly the predecessors had (used) many ways for accomplishing this obligation
and accomplishing one of those ways without specification was obligatory. Then all those ways except one ceased, and therefore that particular way became necessary.

(Likewise) the *salaf* tended not to write down the *Hadith*. The recording of *Hadith* in our time then became necessary as without acquaintance with these books there is no (other) way of (getting access) to the transmission of *Hadith*. The *salaf* did not concern themselves with grammar and language (because) their language was Arabic and so they did not need these arts. However in our age learning Arabic language became necessary because of the distance of period from that of the earlier Arabs.

In short there are too many instances to be presented in support of what we are discussing here. On this basis it is appropriate to draw analogy of the necessity of *taqlid* to a particular imam because sometimes this would be necessary and sometimes this would not be necessary[77]. For instance if an ignorant man lives in India or Transoxiana and there is neither a Shafi'i, Maliki, or Hanbali scholar, nor a book of any of these *madhahib*, (in such circumstances) it becomes necessary for him to observe *taqlid* to the *madhhab* of Abu Hanifa. It is forbidden for him to deviate from his *madhhab* because (in that case) he would be throwing off the noose of the *Shari'a* from his neck and would become a neglected warp.

Contrary to this (situation) would be if he were in *Haramayn*, (then) learning about all the *madhahib* would have been easy for him. There it would not have been sufficient for him to act upon assumption without certainty. Neither should he follow the word of common people nor should he adhere to an unknown book. All that has been explained in (*kitab*) *Al-Nahr al-Fā'iq Sharh Kanz al-Daqā'iq*".

(You should also) know that al-*mujtahid al-mutlaq* is the one who combines five sciences. Al-Nawawi has stated (the following conditions) in *al-Minhāj*. (For *al-mujtahid al-mutlaq* it is necessary that he should be able) to become a judge, be a Muslim, *mukallaf* (legally capable and competent), free, male, just, able to hear, see and speak. (He should also be) competent in exercising *ijtihad* in the laws and that (means) he is conversant with relevant (laws) of the Qur'an and *Sunnah*, its *khāss* and *'ām* (specific and general rules), *mujmal* (ambivalent) and *mubayyin* (detailed) concepts, the abrogator (*nasikh*) and the abrogated (*mansūkh*) (verses). (Likewise he should be well-versed) in *mutawātir Sunnah* and others, *muttasil* and *mursal* (*Ahadith*) and the conditions of strength and weakness in the narrators. (He should also be familiar with) the linguistics and grammar of Arabic, views of the *'ulama'* among the Companions and those after them and (where these views contain) consensus, disagreement and different kinds of analogy".

You should (also) know that this *mujtahid* could be *mustaqil* and could be affiliated to *mustaqil*. *Al-mujtahid al-mustaqil* is the one who is distinguished from the rest of the *mujtahids* in three qualities just as is clearly noticeable in Shafi'i.

Firstly, he should act independently in those principles and rules from which *Fiqh* is deduced. This has been mentioned in the beginning of (*kitab*) *al-Umm* (by Imam Shafi'i), where he has enumerated the works of predecessors in their deductions and (which) were complemented by him.

We have been informed by our Shaikh Abu Tahir Muhammad b. Ibrahim al-Madani, from his Shaikh al-Makkīyy"īn Shaikh Hasan b. 'Ali al-'Ujaimī and Shaikh Ahmad al-Nakhalī, from Shaikh Muhammad b. al-'Ulā' al-Babalī, from Ibrahim b. Ibrahim al-Laqani and 'Abd al-Ra'ūf al-Tiblāwī, from Jalāl al-Din Abu'l-Fadl al-Suyūtī, from Abu'l-Fadl al-Marjani *ijāza* (the permission to narrate *Hadith*), from Abu'l-Faraj al-Ghuzzī, from Yūnus b. Ibrahim al-Dabūsī, from Abu'l-Hasan b. al-Muqīr, from Fadl b. Sahl al-Isfra'īnī, from Hafiz al-Hujja Abu Bakr Ahmad b. 'Ali al-Khatīb, (as saying): "We are told by Abu Na'īm al-Hafiz (that) Abu Muhammad 'Abd Allah b. Muhammad b. Ja'far b. Haddan told (that) 'Abd Allah b.

Muhammad b.Ya'qūb told us (that) Abu Hatim i.e. al-Razi told us (that) Yūnus b. 'Abd al-A'la told us as saying (that) Muhammad b. Idris Shafi'i said: "The Foundation is the Qur'an and *Sunnah*, and if that is not available then by analogy to both of them. And if *Hadith* is (in) uninterrupted (chain of transmission) from the Messenger of Allah (SAAS) and the chains of authorities (of *Hadith*) from him are authentic then it is the *Sunnah*".

The (value of) consensus (among *Fuqaha'* and *mujtahidīn)* is greater than the tradition narrated on the authority of single transmitter (*al-Khabar al-Mufrad*). The *Hadith* is (to be interpreted) according to its literal meaning and if it has the likelihood of (several) meanings, then whichever is more similar to its literal sense, he should interpret it accordingly. And if *Ahadith* are on par with each other then the most authentic one in chains of authorities is the first one. The *(Hadith) al-munqati'* has no standing except that of Ibn al-Musayyab. No principle should be judged by analogy with another principle. With regard to the principle, (questions of) why and how are not asked. On the contrary a secondary matter (*al-far'*) is to be subjected to why? If its analogy with the principle is judged correctly then it (too) is sound and the evidence is established on its basis". (Here) ends (Shafi'i's statement).

Secondly, he *(mujtahid)* should collect *Ahadith* and *athar* so that he may learn their laws and become aware of the sources of *Fiqh* therein. He should (also) reconcile between the inconsistent traditions and give preference to some of them over others and determine some of their probabilities. In our opinion this is nearly one-third knowledge of Shafi'i, and Allah knows best.

Thirdly, he should derive those sub-divisions (*tafarī'*) which are presented to him and which have been not answered before during the (past) centuries acknowledged for (their) virtues. In general by virtue of these qualities he will have the multitude of
disposition, excel his companions, win the race of competition, and become prominent in his field.

The fourth quality that follows this is that acceptance descends for him from the heaven. And so as a result groups of scholars including commentators, traditionists, legists and scholars (*huffaz*) of books of *Fiqh* turn to his knowledge. Then on that acceptance and response long-stretched centuries are passed till it penetrates deeply into the hearts (of the people).

Al-mujtahid al-mutlaq al-muntasib is the one who follows (someone) and is faultless in the first quality (mentioned above) and who follows him (his Shaikh) in his footstep in the second quality. And *al-mujtahid fi'l-madhhab* is the one who is faultless in the first and second (qualities), and gives similar treatment in deriving *tafarī'* on the pattern of his (Shaikh's) *tafarī'*.

Let us quote an example for this purpose. We say: "Any one who in these late times wants to become a doctor has to follow the doctors of Greece or those of India because he is in the position of *al-mujtahid al-mustaqil*. Then if through his own understanding this physician becomes familiar with characteristics of medicines, various diseases, method of making syrups and electuaries (to such an extent) that he becomes aware of that (field) with the help of their direction. (At this stage he) becomes certain of his position without *taqlid* and becomes capable of doing (things by himself) just as they (used to) do. Consequently he becomes familiar with characteristics of those medicines, which had been not spoken of before and explains causes of diseases, their symptoms and remedies, which were not encountered by predecessors. Thus he competes with predecessors over some of the things they had spoken about (whether it is) little or more. So he is in the position of *al-mujtahid al-mutlaq al-muntasib* even though he is more flawless than them without complete certainty. His main concern was to prepare syrups and electuaries on the basis of those established rules like most of the unqualified doctors of these later times do. And so he would be in the position of *al-mujtahid fi'l-madhhab*.

Similarly any one who composes verse in these times has to follow for that purpose either the poetry of Arabs and adopt their meters, rhymes and styles of their odes, or (to follow) the poetry of non-Arabs. Thus he would be in the position of *al-mujtahid al-mustaqil*. Then if this poet invents varieties in erotic poetry, love song, eulogy, satire, admonition and produces the most wonderful things in metaphors and figures of speech and the likes of which have never been (made) before. Not only that but he becomes aware of those things through some of their (predecessors') making, and compares the precedent against (another) precedent and judges one thing against another by way of analogy. (So he) becomes capable of inventing a meter not spoken of before, or a new style such as composition of *mathnawi*[78], *ruba'īya*[79] and observance of rhyming word of a poem, i.e. a complete word that he repeats in each verse after the rhyme all that is done in Arabic poetry, so he is in the position of *al-mujtahid al-mutlaq al-muntasib*. If he is not an inventor but merely follows their methods, then he is in the position of *al-mujtahid fi'l-madhhab*, and the same goes for the science of Qur'anic exegesis, mysticism and other sciences.

If you ask: "Why did the predecessors did not speak very much about the Principles of Jurisprudence, (but) when Shafi'i appeared he spoke about it comprehensively, proficiently and excellently". (In response) I say that this is because everyone among the predecessors used to have the collection of *Ahadith* and *āthār* of his town but did not have the collection of *Ahadith* of the (whole) country. Whenever there appeared contradiction among the evidences of *Ahadith* of his town, he would give his judgement on that contradiction according to the discernment available to him. During the time of Shafi'i, *Ahadith* of (the whole) country were collected together, and as a consequence there appeared contradiction twice in *Ahadith* of the (whole) country and the selections of its *Fuqaha'*: Once between the *Ahadith* of his town and those of another town, and once within the *Ahadith* of the same town.

So everyone supported his *shaikh* according to the discernment he perceived[80]. (As a result) the rift became widened and the dissension increased, and every kind of disagreement was inflicted upon the people on an unprecedented scale. They became confused and puzzled and could not find the way out until the aid of their Lord arrived. Shafi'i was inspired (by Allah) with rules (of *Fiqh*) through which he reconciled between the inconsistent and contradictory (*Ahadith*). Thus he opened a nice door for his successors.

After the third century the (position of) *al-mujtahid al-mutlaq al-muntasib* in the *madhhab* of Imam Abu Hanifa became extinct. This is because only an exceptionally brilliant *muhaddith* (transmitter of *Hadith*) could (hold this position), while their (Hanafi *Fuqaha*'s) involvement in the Science of *Hadith* in past and present has been minimal. They were only *mujtahidun fi'l-madhhab*. This (type of) *ijtihad* was meant by those who maintained 'minimum condition for (becoming a) *mujtahid* was memorisation of (*kitab*) *al-Mabsūt*.

As for *al-mujtahid al-muntasib* in the *madhhab* of Imam Malik and all those of similar stature such as Abu 'Umar known as Ibn 'Abd al-Barr and Qadi Abu Bakr ibn al-'Arabi, they said: "Their unique position in *madhhab* is not regarded as significant in the *madhhab*".

As for the *madhhab* of (Imam) Ahmad (b. Hanbal), it was small (in following) in past and present, and it had *mujtahidūn* generation after generation until it became extinct in the ninth century. (Thus) the (influence of his) *madhhab* dwindled in many countries except for a few people in Egypt and Baghdad.

The position of the *madhhab* of (Imam) Ahmad in relation to the *madhhab* of (Imam) Shafi'i is like that of the *madhhab* of (Imam) Abu Yusuf and (Imam) Muhammad (to the *madhhab* of Abu Hanifa). Despite that his *madhhab* was not recorded with the *madhhab* of Shafi'i during the (time of) recording like the *madhhab* of those two was recorded together with the *madhhab* of Abu Hanifa. Therefore, in our view, the two were not considered as one *madhhab* and Allah knows best. And the recording of his *madhhab* together with his (Shafi'i's) *madhhab* is not difficult (to understand) for the one who had studied about them both in their (proper) way.

As for the *madhhab* of Shafi'i, of all the *madhahib* it has had more frequently *mujtahid mutlaq* and *mujtahid fi'l-madhhab*. Among all the *madhahib* it is the most principled, scholastic and abounding in interpretation of the Qur'an and explanation of *Ahadith*. It is the most sound in chains of authorities and narration, and the strongest of all in (accurately) preserving the texts of the Imam. It is the most vehement in differentiating between the views of the Imam and those of (his) prominent companions, and the most careful in giving preference to some of the views and prominent persons over others. All this is well known to those who study the *madhahib* and are involved in them.

His immediate companions used to apply *ijtihad al-mutlaq* and none of them imitated him in all his *mujtahadāt* (efforts of *ijtihad*) until Ibn Suraij appeared. He established the rules of *taqlid* and *takhrij*. Then came his companions who walked on his path and followed his pattern, and therefore he is regarded as one of the reformers at the beginning of the two centuries, and Allah knows best.

As for Bukhari, although he was affiliated to Shafi'i and agreed with him in most of (the principles of) *Fiqh*, he disagreed with him in many things. (But) what he did on his own is not considered as part of Shafi'i's *madhhab*. As for Abu Dawud and al-Tirmidhi, both of them are *mujtahids* affiliated to Ahmad (b. Hanbal) and Ishaq, and similarly we think of Ibn Majah and al-Darimi, and Allah knows best.

It should also be known to him (the one involved in *Fiqh*) that the subject matter of Shafi'i's *madhhab* consists of *Ahadith* and *athar* (and which are) recorded, well known and used (as original sources). This kind (of distinction) is not found in any other *madhhab*. Among the constituents of his *madhhab* is *kitab al-Muwatta* (of Imam Malik). Although it was earlier than Shafi'i, he based his *madhhab* on it. (Likewise are) *Sahih al-Bukhari, Sahih Muslim,* and the books of Abu Dawūd, al-Tirmidhi, Ibn Majah and al-Darimi, then *Musnad* of Shafi'i, *Sunan* of Nasa'ī, *Sunan* of Dara Qutnī, *Sunan* of Baihaqi and *Sharh al-Sunnah* of Baghawi.

As for Muslim and Abu'l-'Abbas al-Asamm (d. 246AH/860AD) the compiler of *Musnad al-Shafi'i* and (*kitab*) *al-Umm*, and those mentioned by us after him, are devoted to the *madhhab* of Shafi'i, and they all adhere to the same principles. And if you take note of what we have mentioned it will become clear to you that whoever opposes the *madhhab* of Shafi'i will be deprived from the office of *al-ijtihad al-mutlaq*. (It is also worth noting) that the Science of *Hadith* has declined to benefit the one who does not try to study under Shafi'i and his companions.

(Verse)

"And be their sponger with good manners because I don't think a Shafi'i (could be a Shafi'i) without good manners".

The attitude of people towards *Fiqh* after the 4th century

Then after these centuries there appeared other people who went right and left and as a result many things happened among them. (These) include disputation and disagreement over the science of *Fiqh*. Its details according to what has been mentioned by al-Ghazali are as follows. When the reign of the *'rightly guided Caliphs'* ended, the Caliphate came into the hands of people who seized it without entitlement and independence. They didn't have the knowledge of *fatwa* and (Islamic) laws, and were therefore forced to seek the help of *Fuqaha'* and maintain links with them in all the circumstances.

However, there were still some *'ulama'* who maintained their attachment to the *'earlier pattern'* and preserved the purity of Faith. Whenever they were approached (by the authorities) they would run away. (The fact that) despite their avoidance they were sought after by the leaders, was seen by (other) people of those times as a sign of respect of *'ulama'*. This imbued them with quest of knowledge to gain respect and fame. As a result the *Fuqaha'* became petitioners after they were much sought after and despised after they were respectable by turning away from rulers except for those before them (who were) blessed by Allah.

(As a result some) people wrote books on scholastic theology, increased prattling, criticism and counter-criticism and paved the way for disputation. This raised their status in the sight of rulers and kings. Some of those rulers and kings were inclined towards debating (the issues of) *Fiqh* and explaining the precedence of the *madhhab* of Shafi'i and Abu Hanifa. Hence for such people this involvement became their main preoccupation. The result was that people gave up (interest in) scholastic theology and (other) fields of knowledge, and turned their attention to controversial issues, in particular between Shafi'i and Abu Hanifa. They became less concerned with differences between Malik, Sufyan, Ahmad b. Hanbal and others.

They thought their main purpose was to deduct minute details of *Shari'a*, confirm the causes of *madhhab* and to establish the principles of *fatwa,* and so they produced prolific writings and deductions. For this purpose they arranged (various) kinds of argumentation and writings, which they continue to do until this day. We don't know what Allah has determined for the coming times. This is the end of the summary of (al-Ghazali's) statement.

Behold that I found most of them believe that the cause of disagreement between Abu Hanifa and Shafi'i is based on these principles mentioned in the book (*Kanz al-Wusul*) of Bazdawi (d. 482AH/1089AD). On the contrary most of these (principles) have actually been derived from their views. In my opinion the proposed formula that *khass* is clear and does not need to be affixed by explanation (*bayan*), addition (*ziyada*) is abrogation, '*āmm* (general rules of Qur'an) is definitive (*qat'ī*) like *khass*, preference (*tarjīh*) should not be given (to an issue) on the basis of the majority of narrators, when the door of *ra'i* (analogy) is closed, action on *Hadith* (reported) by a non-*Faqih* is not obligatory, as a principle implication of the condition (*mafhūm al-shart*)[81] and implication of the attribute (*mafhūm al-wasf*)[82] should not be taken into account, the reason necessitating the matter is definitely the obligation, and instances like these are in fact the derived principles based on the statements of the imams. Therefore reporting them on the authority of Abu Hanifa and his two companions is not correct. (Similarly) to maintain them and take trouble in responding to criticism over them has not been the practice of predecessors in their inference just as Bazdawi and others do. (And this attitude is not) more worthy than preserving what is contrary to it and answering to the criticism put to him (*Faqih*).

For example they made the principle that '*khass* is clear and (therefore) should not be affixed by explanation. But they went against it in the practice of predecessors with regard to the Qur'anic verse: "Bow down and prostrate yourselves (in prayer)[83], and the saying of the Prophet (SAAS)" The prayer of man is not valid until he straightens his back in bowing and prostration"[84]. This is because they did not speak of the necessity of stillness (of back in bowing and prostration); neither did they treat the *Hadith* as explanation of the verse. As a result their attitude was subjected to criticism in respect of the Qur'anic verse, "And rub your heads (with water in *wudū*)"[85], and rubbing of forelock by the Prophet (SAAS), whereas they treated it as explanation (of the verse).[86] (Similarly), the (following) Qur'anic verses: (i)"The woman and the man guilty of fornication, flog (them)".[87], (ii) "As to the thief, male or female"[88], and (iii) "Until she has married another husband"[89], and the explanations attached to these (verses) afterwards. Therefore, they took great trouble to answer (to the criticism) just as has been mentioned in their books.

They made the principle that *'āmm* is definitive like *khāss*. But they went against it in the attitude of predecessors with regard to the Qur'anic verse: "So you read from Qur'an as much as may be easy for you"[90], and the saying of the Prophet (SAAS): "No prayer is valid without the Opening chapter of Qur'an"[91]. This is because they did not specify it.

(Similarly) with regard to the following saying of the Prophet (SAAS): "Tithe (*'ushr*) is due on what is irrigated by fountainheads", and his saying, "In less than five *awsaq*[92] there is no *sadaqa*"[93], because they did not specify this and other things of this kind. Then the following Qur'anic verse was cited against them "Send an offering for sacrifice, such as you may find"[94]; on the contrary it is the goat and (animals) bigger than it, because of the explanation (made) by the Prophet (SAAS). And so they resorted to mannerism to find the answer.

Similarly they made the principle that *mafhūm al-shart wa'l-wasf* does not deserve any consideration, (but) stepped out of their own attitude about the Qur'anic verse: "If any of you does not have the means"[95]. Then most of their actions went against them such as the saying of the Prophet (SAAS) "Zakah is due on camels (which) graze freely", and as a result they took pains to answer. They (also) made the principle that it is not obligatory to act upon a *Hadith* (narrated) by a non-*Faqih* when the door of *ra'i* has been closed and went out of their own principle in respect of abandoning *Hadith al-musarrāt*. Then they were subjected to criticism with regard to their attitude to *Hadith* of *qahqaha* (loud burst of laughter), and the *Hadith* about invalidity of the fast for unintentional eating, and so they took trouble to answer.

There are many examples of what we have mentioned and which are not unknown to the one who follows up, and the one who does not follow up, long (discussion) will not benefit him let alone a brief hint. As evidence to this, it will suffice you to refer to the view of research scholars. Accordingly, if there appears an issue (*mas'ala*) it is not obligatory to act upon the *Hadith* (narrated) by the one (who is) known for accuracy, retention (*dabt*) and fairness but not (known for) *Fiqh* and (also) when the door of *ra'i* has been closed such as *Hadith al-musarrat*. This is the *madhhab* of 'Isa b. Abān which has been adopted by many later (scholars).

(However), Karkhi, followed by many *'ulama'*, believed in non-stipulation of *Fiqh* for transmitter because of the precedence of *Hadith* over analogy. They maintained that this view was not reported from their (predecessor) companions. On the contrary it was reported from them that *khabar wahid* has the precedence over analogy. Didn't you realise that they (*Fuqaha'*) acted upon the *Hadith* (reported by) Abu Hurairah about the fasting person who eats or drinks unintentionally? Although it is contrary to analogy, Abu Hanifa said: "If it were not for (this) report I would have supported the analogy". In this respect you may also be guided by *Fuqaha's* differences over most of their deductions by inference from their own actions and refutation of one another.

I found some of the *Fuqaha'* believe that all that is found in these elaborate commentaries and huge books of *fatawa* is the view of Abu Hanifa and his two companions, without making difference between the deduced view and the actual view of Abu Hanifa. Neither does their statement carry the meaning that 'according to the *takhrīj* of Karkhi is so and so and according to the *takhrīj* of Tahawī (Abu Ja'far Ahmad b. Sulaiman al-Azdi d.321AH/ 933AD) is so and so. Nor does distinction appear between their statement (that) Abu Hanifa said so-and so and between their statement (that) 'answer to the question according to the view of Abu Hanifa is so-and-so. Attention is also not given to what the Hanafi research scholars like Ibn al-Humam and Ibn Nujaim (al-Hanafi d. 970AH/ 1563AD) have said concerning the issue of *al-'ashr fi'l 'ashr*.[96], and the question of distance of one mile from water for *tayammum*. Examples like these (show) that such things are the *takhrījāt* of companions and not actually a *madhhab*.

I (also) found some of them believe that the foundation of *madhhab* is based on these polemical arguments mentioned in *Mabsūt* of Sarakhsī (Shams al-Din Abu Bakr Muhammad b. Sahl d. 483AH/1090AD), *al-Hidāya* (of Abu'l-Hasan 'Ali b. Abu Bakr al-Marghīnānī d. 593AH/1196AD) and *al-Tabyīn* (*al-Haqā'iq Sharh Kanz al-Daqā'iq* of 'Uthman b.'Ali Al-Zayla'ī d.743AH/1342AD) and (other books) like these. They don't know that the first (people) among whom such (kinds of things) appeared were the *Mu'tazila* but their *madhhab* is not based upon it. Then the later (scholars) found it appealing for broadening and sharpening the minds of students or for (reasons) other than that, and Allah knows best. Most of these ambiguities and doubts belong to what we have clearly stated in this book.

I (also) found some of them believe that there is no third sect other than *Zāhiriyya* and *Ahl al-Ra'i*, and that anyone who applies analogy and inference belongs to *Ahl al-Ra'i*. Not at all by Allah. On the contrary *ra'i* does not mean the same understanding and sense because no scholar is dispense with it. Neither that *ra'i* which does not in principle rely on *Sunnah* has any basis, because no Muslim definitely subscribes to it. Nor (*ra'i* means) the ability of deduction and analogy because there has been consensus that Ahmad and Ishaq and even Shafi'i did not belong to *Ahl al-Ra'i*, but despite that they applied inference and analogy.

On the contrary *Ahl al-Ra'i* means a people who after (studying) the issues agreed upon among the Muslims or among the majority of them, turned their attention to the (process of) deduction in accordance with the principles of the earlier (scholars). Most of their work was interpretation of precedent in the sense of precedent. They used to refer to one of the principles (of *Fiqh* when faced with an issue) without (trying to) search for *Ahadith* and *athar* (on that issue).

As for a *Zāhirī*, he is the one who advocates neither analogy nor *athar* of the Companions and Followers. They are people like Dawud b. Hazm and in between these two (sects) are people of *Ahl al-Sunnah* like Ahmad and Ishaq.

As a consequence of these (assumptions) they became content with *taqlid* and it crept in their hearts like the creeping of ant, which they did not realise. This was due to rivalry and disputation among the *Fuqaha'*. This was because whenever they vied with each other over (giving) a *fatwa*, anyone who gave *fatwa* concerning something had his *fatwa* contradicted and disproved. The wrangling continued until the matter was referred to the comment of an earlier (scholar) regarding the issue.

It was also because of the injustice of judges. When most of them deviated from justice and were no longer trustworthy, nothing was approved of them except that which did not cause suspicion in minds of the common people and which could have been something dealt with before.

It was also due to the ignorance of the leaders. The people used to seek *fatwa* from those who had no knowledge of *Hadith* or the method of deduction. You may find this (phenomenon) evident among most of the later (scholars), which has been pointed out by Ibn al-Humam and others. In those days a *non-mujtahid* was called *Faqih* and the *Fuqaha'* of that age remained firm on partisanship.

In fact most of the differences among *Fuqaha'* were over issues over where the views of the Companions (supported) both sides. For example, *takbirāt al-tashriq*.[97], *takbirat al-'idain, nikah al-mahram*[98], *tashshud* of Ibn 'Abbas and Ibn Mas'ud[99] utterance of *'amin*[100], recitation of words twice or once in *iqama*, (*al-intifā' wa'l-ītār*). (Such differences) were merely over giving precedence to either of the two views. In principle the *salaf* did not differ over the issue being related to *Shari'a*. On the contrary their differences were over which of the two matters was more worthy. An example of this is the disagreement between *Qurrā'* (Reciters of Qur'an) over the forms of recitation (of Qur'an).

In this respect they (the *salaf*) argued a lot maintaining that (even though) the Companions had differences, they were all on the right path. So therefore the *'ulama'* still approve of the *fatawa* of *muftis* in respect of the issues involving *ijtihad*, and accepted the decisions of the judges and in some cases acted against their own *madhhab*.

Therefore you will notice that the imams of *madhahib* in such situations affirm the view (of other imams). They used to acknowledge the disagreement by making (such) remarks "This is the most cautious, and this is the adopted view (*mukhtār*) and this is most desirable to me", and would say: "Nothing except that has reached us". These (kind of examples) can be found in abundance in *al-Mabsut*, (*kitab*) *al-Āthār* of Muhammad (b. al-Hasan) and the statement of Shafi'i.

Then after them came successors who condensed the views of the people (before them). They strengthened the disagreement by firmly sticking to the adopted view of their imams, which reported (to them) from the *salaf* of the emphasis on adherence to the *madhhab* of their companions and that in no circumstances they should abandon it. Obviously this (attitude) is natural, because everyone likes what is the choice of his companions even in respect of clothes and foods. Or (this attitude was prevalent) due to the contention arising out of the observance of proof and for (other) reasons like that. As a result some of them assumed (these differences) by way of prejudice and temptation, and they were far beyond than that.

Some of the Companions, Followers and those (who came) after them used to recite *basmala*, while among them there were those who did not recite it; some of them used to read it loudly and others did not read it loudly. Some of them read *qunūt*[101] in *Fajr* (prayer) while others did not read it in *Fajr* (prayer). Among them there were those who used to perform ablution because of cupping, nose bleeding and vomiting, while others did not make *wudū* because of those things. Some of them performed *wudū* for lustfully touching the penis and women, while others would not perform *wudū* because of such things. Some of them used to perform *wudū* for eating the meat of camel while others did not perform *wudū* because of that. Despite (all these differences) they used to pray behind each other. For example, Abu Hanifa, his companions, Shafi'i and others prayed behind the imams of Madina (who were) Malikites and of other inclinations, even though they did not read *basmala* (in prayers), secretly or loudly.

(Once Harun) al-Rashid led the prayer after being cupped, and Imam Abu Yusuf prayed behind him (but) did not repeat (the prayer). He (the former) was given *fatwa* by Imam Malik that (in this situation) *wudū* was not necessary for him. Imam Ahmad b. Hanbal considered *wudu* (necessary) because of nose bleeding and cupping. He was asked: "If the imam had the bleeding and did not perform *wudū* (afterwards), would you pray behind him?" He replied: "Why shouldn't I pray behind Imam Malik and Sa'id b. al-Musayyab?"

It is reported that Abu Yusuf and Muhammad used to say *takbīr* in *'idain* (prayers) on the pattern of Ibn 'Abbas because Harun al-Rashid liked the *takbīr* of his grandfather. (When) Shafi'i prayed the Morning Prayer near the mausoleum of Abu Hanifa; he did not read *qunūt* (as a token) of respect. He also said: "Perhaps we have descended to the *madhhab* of the people of 'Iraq". Malik said (the same) to Mansur and Harun al-Rashid what we have (already) mentioned about him before.

It is reported in (*kitab*) *al-Bazāzīah* (of Muhammad b. Shihab b. Bazāz d. 827 A.H.) about the second Imam i.e. Abu Yusuf, that after bathing in public bath he led the people in Friday (prayer). After he finished the prayer and the people dispersed, he was informed of a dead mouse in the well of the bath. In response, he said: "In that case we will follow the view of our Madinian brethren, (which says): "When the water reaches *qullatain* it does not get impure". Here (ends the statement).

Among these (kinds of differences) was (also) that most of them (*Fuqaha'*) focused on minute details of every field. Some of them claimed that they intend to establish the science of Biography, Chronology and the degrees of Criticism and Fairness of Narrators of Hadith (*Asmā' al-Rijāl wa ma'rifat marātib al-Jarh wa'l-ta'dīl*), (but) then from there they drifted into the history, past and present. Some of them investigated about the rare and *gharīb* traditions but ended up with fabricated *Ahadith* (*mawdū'*). Some of them increased palaver over the Principles of Jurisprudence and everyone deduced disputatious rules of polemics in support of (the view of) his companions. They cited (them), investigated them and thoroughly examined them, answered (to the objection and criticism over them), defined (the subject) and divided (it into chapters). Sometimes they wrote detailed statement and sometimes epitomised them.

Some of the *Fuqaha'* went too far in assuming the improbable conditions which even do not deserve the attention of a sensible person. They liked getting involved into the generalities (*'umūmāt*) and indications (*īma'āt*) from the statements of those involved in deduction and others, which neither a scholar nor an ignorant would like to listen to. The dissension (*fitna*) of this disputation, disagreement and indulgence is nearly the same as that of the first *fitna* when they (Muslims) disputed with each other over the (question) of government and every one supported his companion. So just as that (*fitna*) resulted in mordacious rule, deaf and blind events, similarly this (*fitna*) ensued ignorance, confusion, doubts and illusion, which has no boundaries.

As a consequence after them there arose generations upon mere *taqlid*. They did not discern truth from falsehood and inference from polemic. So in those days he (was considered) *Faqih* who was prattle braggart and who had unwittingly memorised the strong and weak statements of *Fuqaha'*. He would set them forth with the twitter of his both jawbones. And *muhaddith* was (regarded the one) who enumerated *Ahadith* (both) sound and infirm, and reported them deliriously like the raving of nightly chats with (full) strength of his both jawbones.

I don't describe that (condition) as a general practice, because among the servants of Allah there is a group (of people) whom it does not matter whoever humiliates them. They are '*the evidence of Allah on His earth*' even though they are in small number. Thereafter came no generation but it was most dissentful, abound in *taqlid* and stronger in stripping the trust from the hearts of the people. (This attitude became so much widespread) that they became content with abandoning involvement in the affairs of religion. They would say:

"We found our fathers following a certain religion and we will certainly follow in their footsteps"[102]. It is Allah to whom complaint is made and He is the one whose help is sought and upon Him lies reliance". This is the end of what we wanted to mention in this treatise entitled "*Al-Insaf fi bayan sabab al-ikhtilaf*". Praise be to Allah before and after, in openness and secret. May (this work) be accomplished with blessing and relief.

Bibliography

Amin S.H.

Arabic-English Dictionary of legal terms, compiled by Mary C. Armstrong, Royston Publishers, Glasgow, 1990.

'Asqalani, Ahmad b. Hajar.

Fath al-Bārī Sharh Sahīh al-Bukhārī, ed. Muhibb al-Din al-Khatib, Al-Maktaba al-Salafiya, Cairo: 1407 A.H.

Azami, Dr. Muhammad Mustafa.

Studies in Early Hadith Literature. 2nd edn. Indianapolis: American Trust Publications. 1978.

Bukhari, Muhammad b. Isma'il.

Sahih al-Bukhārī. Eng. trans. Muhammad Muhsin Khan. 9 vols, Qazi Publications, Lahore: 1979.

Al-Dihlawi, Shah 'Abd al-Haqq Muhaddith.

Ashi''a al-Lam'āt Sharh Mishkāt, Urdu translation and footnotes. Muhammad Sa'id Ahmad Naqshbandi. 6 Vols. Fareed Bookstall, Lahore, 1981-86

Al-Dihlawi, Shah Wali Allah.

Hujjat Allah al-Bāligha. (Part 1 & 2), ed. Al-Sayyad Sabiq. Cairo: Dar al-Kutub al-Haditha, 1322 A.H.

Encyclopaedia of Islam. New edn. E.J.Brill, Leiden, 1983.

Ibn Manzur, Al-Ansari.

Lisan al-'Arab, 1st edn. Dar al-Fikr, Bayrut, 1410/ 1990.

Ibn al-Salah.

Muqaddama Ibn al-Salah wa Mahāsin al-Istilah, ed. Dr. A'isha bint al-Shati'.

Dar al-Ma'arif, Cairo, 1409/ 1989.

Kamali, Dr. Mohammad Hashim.

Principles of Islamic Jurisprudence, (Revised edn.), Islamic Texts Society, Cambridge, 1991.

Lane, E. W.

An Arabic-English Lexicon, 8 pts. London, 1963-93.

Maududi, Syed Abu'l- A'la.

Tajdīd u Ihya'i Dīn, 5th edn. Islamic Publications, Lahore, 1960.

Al-Mawsū'a al-Fiqhīyya, (31 Vols.) 4th edn. Ministry of Awqaf and Islamic affairs, Kuwait: 1414 AH/ 1993 AD.

Qazi Javaid.

Afkār Shah Walī Allah, Nigarshat Lahore, H.Y. Printers, Lahore, 1986.

Barrae Saghīr main Muslim Fikr kā irtiqā, Nigarshat Lahore, 1986.

The Holy Qur'an: Text, Translation, and Commentary by 'Abdullah Yusuf 'Ali. Islamic Foundation, Leicester (UK), 1975.

Shaikh Muhammad Ikram.

Rud-e-Kausar, Taj Company, Delhi, 1987.

Sa'idi, Ghulam Rasul.

Sharh Sahih Muslim (Urdu translation and Commentary), 7 vols. Fareed Bookstall, Lahore, 1994-97.

Sir 'Abd ul-Rahim.

Principles of Islamic Jurisprudence, Urdu trans. Maulvi Mas'ud 'Ali: *Usul-i-Fiqhi Islam*, 1st edn. Ali Kamran Publishers, Lahore, 1989.

GLOSSARY

Adab: manners, rules or voluntary acts of conduct observed with the intention of reward and nearness.

Afrād plural of *fard*: chain of *Hadith* (isnad) with only one transmitter at each stage, or a *Hadith* reported only by people of a particular area.

Ahkām plural of *hukm*: rules, Islamic laws.

Al-'ashr fi'l-'ashr: ten by ten. According to a famous *Fiqhi* formula the water of a pool, measuring 10 yards width and 10 yards length, is pure.

Asmā al-Rijāl: biographies of men involved in the transmission of *Hadith*.

Āthār: plural of *athar*, traces, works or traditions. It is applied to both, the *Hadith* of the Prophet (SAAS) and the sayings of the Companions and Followers.

Awsaq plural of *wasq* is equal to sixty *sa's* and one *sa'* is equal to about 3 kilograms.

Fard Kifāya: collective duty in comparison to *Fard 'ain*: individual duty

Fatwa: a decree, a legal or religious opinion given by a Mufti/ religious authority often in response to an enquiry.

Furū' plural of far': branches, subsidiary or secondary matters, derived from the principles of Islamic Law.

Furūd plural of *fard*: Obligations/duties or essential aspects of Islam such as observance of ablution for prayer.

Gharīb from *gharaba*: something strange or rare. It is applied to a *Hadith* which is reported from only one Companion or which is transmitted at a later stage by a single transmitter.

Ghurra: blood money.

Hadith Maqlūb (transposed) is applied when a tradition is attributed to someone other than the real authority to make it an acceptable *gharib* tradition, or when two traditions have the *isnad* of the one with the *matn* of the other.

Huffaz plural of *hafiz*: the one who preserves or learns something by heart. A traditionist who remembers one hundred thousand or more reported *Ahadith* together with their *matn* and *sanad* and the conditions of *jarh* and *ta'dil* (criticism and authentication).

Ibāha: permissibility.

'Iddah: a woman's period of waiting after divorce or death of her husband during which she is not allowed to remarry.

Ihlāl: to assume *ihram* for *'umra* or *hajj*.

Ijtihad: independent judgement given by a jurist in deducting a rule on the basis of Qur'an or *Sunnah*.

Ikhtilaf: disagreement, difference of opinion among the jurists over the interpretation of a matter of law.

Īmā': signs or indications found in a speech of text.

Iqtidā al-Nass: alluded meaning of the text.

'Illa: literally cause, reason of a law or religious injunction. It also means an ailment in *Hadith*.

Al-Intifā': repetition of words in *iqama* in contrast to ***itar*** where they are read once.

Isnad or *sanad*: chains of reporters of *Hadith*.

Iqama: the second call for prayer, which is made to announce that the congregational prayer is about to begin.

Istidlal: judicial reasoning/ argument.

Istifta': consultation, an inquiry made to a *mufti*.

Istihsan: juristic inquiry, methods of reasoning, application of discretion in a legal decision as a result of personal deliberation.

Istinja: answering the call of nature and cleansing of private parts afterwards.

Ittisāl: of *Isnad* going back to the Prophet (SAAS) without interruption, while *inqita'* means interruption in *isnad*.

Al-Jahr bi'l-basmala: recitation of Bis *millah al-Rahman al-Rahim* loudly in prayer in contrast to *al-ikhfa' bi'l-basmala*.

Al-Jam' bain al-Mukhtalifain: reconciliation between two (or more) inconsistent or controversial *Ahadith*.

Junub from *janaba*: the state of ritual impurity caused by sexual intercourse or a nocturnal discharge in a wet dream.

Khabar Wahīd: a tradition reported by a single person.

Khiyār al-Majlis: choice of confirming or cancelling a deal in a business meeting.

Madhhab: an opinion, a school of thought, usually referred to one of the schools of Islamic Jurisprudence.

Mahr: bridal money or things given or promised to be given to wife by her husband on wedding.

Mansūs: clear textual injunction of Qur'an or *Hadith*.

Makrūh: a reprehensible, undesirable or objectionable act. In *fiqh* it is applied to something disapproved of but not forbidden.

Marfū' Muttasil: *Muttasil* is used for an unbroken *isnad* traced back to the source. If it goes back to the Prophet (SAAS) it is *muttasil marfu'*, if to a Companion it is *muttasil mawquf*.

Mathnawi: a poem in which the second line of each distich rhymes with the same letter.

Mawqūf: a *Hadith* accredited back to a Companion.

Mubayyīn: clear, unambiguous injunctions of Qur'an.

Mufrid: (from *ifrad*) the one who puts on *ihram* with the intention of performing *hajj* only and does not perform *'umra*.

Mufti: a religious scholar who is competent in Islamic sciences in particular *fiqh* and is therefore qualified to give *fatwa*.

Muhaqala: a forbidden sale of grain not fully-grown and ripe against fully-grown grain.

Muhkam: a word the meaning of which is fixed, a confirmed and unabrogated injunction of Qur'an or *Hadith*.

Mujmal: general injunctions or meanings of Qur'an.

Mujtahid: the one who endeavours, a *faqih* who after gaining command in religious sciences, in particular *fiqh*, becomes authorized to give independent judgement on religious issues.

Mujtahid Mutlaq: a jurist with absolute power of exposition.

Munāzara: debate and discussion on an issue.

Munkar: literally reprehensible. A *Hadith* similar to *Shadhah* except that the reporter who goes against other reporters in his report is not trustworthy. Hence such report is to be rejected.

Munqati'*:* a *Hadith* with an interrupted or discontinued chain of narrators.

Mursal: a *Hadith* in which the name of the Companion reporting the *Hadith* directly from the Prophet (SAAS) is omitted.

Mustahada: a woman who is bleeding in between her menstruation.

Musnad: a *Hadith* which has uninterrupted *isnad* (chains of reporters) from the Prophet (SAAS).

Mustafīda: (from *istafada*) literally means abundance, overflow of water. Technically it is a *Hadith Sahih* which has more than two narrators and it gets widespread currency and acceptability because of the reliability of narrators and the authenticity of *isnad*. Some traditionists treat it as equivalent to *mashhur*; others regard it as equivalent to *mutawatir*.

Mut'a: temporary marriage, it was allowed in the early days of Islam, but later it was abrogated.

Mutamatti' (from *tamattu'*): the one who performs *'umra* before *hajj* with separate *ihrams* for both.

Muwalāt: sequence and continuity, to perform all actions of ablution continuously and in their exact order and sequence.

Muzābana: a forbidden sale in which the dry dates or other such things are sold by way of weight or measure for something of this kind whose weight or measure are not known.

Al-Nafar: an optional practice for pilgrims to stop and relax for a while at *al-abtah*: a mountain path and basin shaped valley while returning to Makkah from Mina.

Nass: a clear and express text/injunction of Qur'an or *Hadith*.

Nikah al-Mahram: those for whom marriage with a woman is forbidden because of kinship relationship such as father, son, brother and others who come in the same category.

Qawā'id plural of *qa'ida*: rules and regulations of Islamic Jurisprudence.

Qarā'in plural of *qarina*: presumptions, circumstantial evidences.

Qārin (from *Qiran*) is the one who combines *hajj* and *'umra* together by performing *'umra* before *hajj* while being in the same state of *ihram* for both.

Qiyas: analogy applied by a jurist in deduction of a rule.

Qunut: a special *du'a* (supplication) offered in *'Isha* or *Fajr* prayer.

Qurba: nearness. Something done voluntarily with the intention of reward.

Ra'i: arbitrary/ subjective opinion used in religious laws.

Ramal :one of the rites of *hajj/ 'umra* during which the pilgrims walk at a quick pace with the fast movement of shoulders and legs.

Rukn: literally pillar, essential part of religion, *wudu* or prayer.

Rubā'īya : a stanza of four lines.

Rujū': to withdraw/ retract from a view/position.

Salaf: literally what happened in the past. It is usually applied to the earlier Muslim generations, in particular the Companions of the Prophet (SAAS), the Followers and the Followers of Followers.

Sahīh: literally correct, a sound /authentic *Hadith*.

Taqlīd: imitation, to follow the view of a founder of a *madhhab* or a renowned *faqih*.

Shādhah: a *Hadith*, which is reported by a trustworthy reporter but differs from what is reported by others.

Tabaqāt plural of *tabaqa*: group or classes of *Fuqaha'* of different *madhahib*.

Tā'mīn: to utter '*amin*' loudly after the imam completes reciting '*al-Fatiha*' in congregational prayer.

Al-Tashrīk: literally means partnership or association. As a technical term of Islamic Jurisprudence it means giving shares of inheritance to full brothers with their maternal brothers.

Tayammum: substitute for ablution done on dry land or sand.

Tawātur: transmission of *Hadith* by so many transmitters in every age that it seems impossible for such a great number to agree on fabrication or falsehood.

Turuq: lines of transmission of *Hadith*.

Al- 'Ushr or tithe: a kind of agricultural tax which is one tenth of the crop produced on land which is collected for public welfare.

Usūl al-fiqh: Principles of Islamic Jurisprudence.

Wājib: obligatory

Index of Qur'anic verses

1. They ask you about the fighting....
2. They ask you about menstruation....
3. It is prescribed upon you when death...
4. Every party rejoices in....
5. If they are pregnant...(f.n)
6. The wives of your sons.... (f.n.)
7. Bow down and....
8. And rub your heads...
9. The woman and the man guilty of....
10. As to the thief...
11. Until she has married...
12. So you read from the Qur'an...
13. Send an offering..........
14. If any of you do not have the means....
15. We found our fathers following....

Index of *Ahadith*

1. It is reported on the authority of Ibn 'Abbas, " I have never seen a people...............
2. It is reported on the authority of 'Abd Allah b. 'Umar, "don't ask that which..........
3. It is reported on the authority of 'Umar b. Ishaq " the Companions of the Messenger of Allah (SAAS)....
4. It is reported on the authority of 'Ubada b. Busr al-Kindi, "a woman who died.........
5. It is reported on the authority of Abu Bakr, " I did not hear.....................
6. *Hadith al-Ghurra* (f.n.)
7. *Hadith al-Waba'* (f.n)
8. *Hadith al-Majus* . (f.n)
9. The report by al-Nasa'i: 'Abd Allah b. Mas'ud was asked about a woman...
10. On the authority of Ma'qal b. Yasar: "testifying that he (SAAS)................
11. Abu Huraira was of the opinion that if............
12. Fatima bint Qays (R.A)) testified before 'Umar ibn al-Khattab (RA) that she was triple divorcee...
13. Bukhari and Muslim report that 'Umar ibn al-Khattab (RA) was of the opinion that for a ritually impure person..........
14. Report by Muslim that Ibn 'Umar (R.A) used to ask women...
15. Report by al-Zuhri that Hind had not known the concession given by the................
16. Abu Huraira and Ibn 'Umar (RA) construed this stopover...
17. Ibn 'Abbas (R.A) believed that the Prophet (SAAS) did *ramal*.

18. Report by Abu Dawud on the authority of Sa'id b. Jubair about the *hajj* of the Prophet (SAAS)...

19. Ibn'Umar used to say: the Messenger of Allah (SAAS) performed *'umra*...

20. Report by Ibn 'Umar or 'Umar that the dead person is chastised...........

21. Hasan b.'Ali said: (Once) a funeral procession of a Jew was passing..................

22. 'Abd Allah b.'Abbas said: the permission (of *mut'a*) was given ....

23. Jabir saw him (SAAS) facing the *Ka'ba*...

24. *Hadith Wulūgh al-Kalb* (f.n.).

25. The *Hadith* "From every (coming) generation just and fair..."

26. The *Hadith* "Truly there is no (right of) bequest for an heir"...

27. The *Hadith al-Qullatain*...

30. The *Hadith Khiyār al-Majlis*...

31. 'Abd Allah b. Mas'ud (said): I dislike making something lawful ....

32. Mu'adh b. Jabal said: O people! Don't hasten on the trial before.............

33. Abu Bakr would say: praise be to Allah who made amongst us...........

34. It is reported on the authority of (Qadi) Shuraih that 'Umar ibn al-Khattab wrote to him..

35. It is reported on the authority of 'Abd Allah b. Mas'ud as saying:..................

36. Whenever 'Abd Allah b. 'Abbas was asked about a matter, he would.............

37. It is reported on the authority of Ibn 'Abbas as saying: "don't you

fear............

38. Qatada is reported to have said: Ibn Sirin told a man a *Hadith*.................

39. Auwza'i is reported to have said: 'Umar b.'Abd al- 'Aziz. wrote........

40. 'Amash said: the *Hadith* related by Samī' al-Zayyat from Ibn 'Abbas...........

41. Tirmidhi reported Abu'l-Sa'ib as saying...........

42. 'Abd Allah b.'Abbas, 'Ata, Mujahid and Malik b. Anas are reported to have said..

43. We have been told that a pious man (SAAS) the Messenger of Allah (SAAS) in his dream...

44. When 'Umar sent a group of *Ansar* to Kufa, he told them...

45. The *Hadith* concerning the prohibition of stringed (musical) instruments...

46. The *Hadith al-Musarrat*...

47. The *Hadith* concerning the annulment of the shares of relatives...

48. The *Hadith*: "The prayer of man is not valid..."

49. And the rubbing of forelock by him (SAAS)...

50. "No prayer is valid without...."

51. "Tithe is due on what is irrigated...."

52. "In less than five *awsaq*..."

53. "Zakah is due on camels..."

Index of Books mentioned in Arabic Text

Ādāb al-Futyā by Ibn al-Salah

Abi Dawūd (Musnad)

Al-Nahr al-Fā'iq Sharh Kanz al-Daqā'iq

Al-Bahr by Al-Royani

Al-Darimī (Sunan)

Fatāwa Ibn al-Salah

Al-Hāwī by al-Mawardī

Al-Hidāya of Al-Marghīnānī

Al-Insāf fi Bayan Sabab al-Ikhtilaf of Shah Wali Allah al-Dihlawi

Ibn Mājah (Sunan)

Jāmi' 'Abd al-Razzaq

Al-Jāmi' al-Kabīr by Imam Muhammad b. Hasan al-Shaibani

Jāmi' al-Sahih al-Bukhari

Kitab al-Anwār

Kitab al-Āthār by Imam Muhammad al-Shaibani

Kitab al-Bazdawī

Kitab al-Mabsūt by Al-Sarakhsi

Kitab al-'Umm by Imam Shafi'i

Ma'ālim al-Sunan by Imam al-Khattabī

Al-Minhāj by Al-Nawawī

Al-Muwatta by Imam Malik

Mukhtasar al-Usūl by Ibn al-Hājib

Musnad Imam Ahmad b. Hanbal

Musnad al-Shafi'i

Al-Insaf fi bayan sabab al-ikhtilaf

Musannaf Abi Bakr b. Shayba

Nuskhah of 'Amr b. Shu'aib

Nuskhah of Burayd

Qūt al-Qulūb by Abu Talib Al-Makki

Al-Radd ila man akhlada ila'l-'ard wa jahila ann'l-ijtihad fard fi kull 'asr: Shah Wali Allah

Sahih al-Bukhari

Sahih Muslim

Al-Sahīhayn

Sharh al-Muhadhdhab by al-Nawawī

Sharh al-Sunnah by al-Baghawī

Sharh al-Tanbīh by Jalāl al-Dīn al-Suyūtī

Al-Sharh al-Wajiz of Al-Ghazali by al-Rafi'i

Sunan Abi Dawud al-Sijistani

Sunan al-Baihaqi

Sunan al-Dara Qutnī

Sunan al-Nasa'ī

Al-Tabaqāt by al-Nawawī

Al-Tabaqāt al-Shafi'īyya al-Kubrā by al-Subki

Al-Tabyīn al-Haqā'iq Sharh Kanz al-Daqā'iq of 'Uthman b. 'Ali Al-Zayla'ī

Al-Tahdhīb by al-Nawawī

Al-Tahrīr by Ibn al-Humām

Al-Tirmidhi (Jami')

Footnotes

1. Although, Salman Farsi (RA) is reported to be the first translator of Qur'an in Persian, a translation of Qur'an in Persian is also attributed to Shaikh Sa'di al-Shirazi. However, its authenticity has remained ambiguous and it never became popular. Before Shah Wali Allah another Indian scholar Malik al-'ulama' Qadi Shihab al-Din Dawlatabadi is known to have written a *tafsir* called Bahr Mawwaj, but it too never became popular. Shaikh M. Ikram, Rud-e Kauthar (Taj Company, Delhi, 1987), p.552.
2. Qazi Javaid, *Afkar Shah Wali Allah*, (Nigarshat Lahore, Lahore, 1986), p.68
3. Ibid. 68. *Taqlid* literally means imitation. In *Fiqh* it means to follow the *madhhab* of an imam or a jurist without questioning his authority or interpretation of the laws.
4. Ibid. .96
5. *Encyclopaedia of Islam*, (1983 edition, Leiden), Vol.2. p.254
6. *Tajdid-u- Ihya'ay Din* (Islamic Publications, Lahore, 1966), pp.89-90
7. Q.Javaid. *op. cit.*, pp.102-104
8. Maududi, *op.cit.,,*, .p. 94
9. Ibid.94
10. Q. Javaid, *op.cit.*p.124 (quotation from Maulana 'Ubaid Ullah Sindhi, Shah *Wali Allah awr unka Falsafa*, pp.76-77)
11. Utterance of *'Bism Allah Al-Rahman Al-Rahim'*
12. Translation of *Al-Tabi'un* i.e. those who follow. It is applied to the second generation of Muslims, especially to the disciples of the Companions.
13. Plural of *mujtahid*, the one who endeavours: a *Faqih* who because of his command in religious sciences, especially *Fiqh* and integrity of character has gained the authority to practise *ijtihad*, that is to give independent judgement on religious issues.
14. *Furu' plural* of far': branches, subsidiary or secondary matters, derived from or based on the principles of Islamic Laws.
15. *Muwalat*: to perform all actions of *ablution* continuously and in their exact order and sequence.
16. *Al-Baqara*: 217
17. *Al-Baqara*: 232
18. *Al-waqa'i'*: day-to-day events, expose of facts in a judgement.
19. In the text it reads Muhammad b. Salama.
20. *Ghurra*: blood money. This refers to a *Hadith* reported on the authority of Hisham from his father who reported it from his father Mughira b. Shu'ba that 'Umar consulted them over the aborted foetus (*imlas al-mar'a*) i.e. *al-siqt* (miscarried foetus). Mughira told him that the Messenger of Allah (SAAS) ruled that the blood money should be paid for it. 'Umar said: "If you are truthful then bring someone who knows that (ruling)". Thereupon Muhammad b. Maslama testified that the Messenger of Allah (SAAS) gave that ruling.. 'Abd Allah al-Dhahabi: *Tadhkira al –Huffaz*, (2nd.edn.Da'ira al-Ma'arif, Hyderabad Dakan, 1333 A.H), vol.1.p.8. This may further refer to a *Hadith* reported on the authority of Abu Hurairah (RA) that two women from the tribe of Hudhail (had a fight), and one of them threw a stone at the other, which caused her miscarriage. The Messenger of Allah (SAAS) ruled that the killer (of the foetus) should free a male or female slave (as *diya*). Cf.

Ahmad b. Hajar al-'Asqalani: *Fath al-Bari Sharh Sahih al-Bukhari,* (3rd.edn. ed. Muhibb al-Din al-Khatib, Al-Maktaba al-Salafiya, Cairo, 1407 A.H), Bab Janin al-Mar'ah, vol.12. p.257.

21 *Al-waba'*: This refers to a *Hadith* narrated by 'Abd Allah b.'Amir that 'Umar went to Syria, and when he reached (a place called) Sargh, he was told that an epidemic of plague has broken out in Syria. 'Abd al-Rahman b.'Awf told him that the Messenger of Allah (SAAS) said: "if you hear that it (plague) has broken out in a land, do not go to it; but if it breaks out in a land where you are present, do not leave it to escape it". *Ibid.* Bab ma yudhkar fi'l-Ta 'un. Vol.10. p.189.

22 This refers to a report mentioned in many works of *Hadith* that 'Umar ibn al-Khattab (R.A) did not impose *jizya* on *Majus* until 'Abd al-Rahman b. 'Awf informed him of the practice of the Prophet (SAAS) as well as his saying: "Treat *Majus* the way *Ahl al-Kitab* are treated ". *Ibid.* Kitab al-Jizya wa'l-Muwada'a, Vol.6.pp 297-8

23 This refers to a *Hadith* reported on the authority of Abu Sa'id al-Khudri as saying: "One day we were sitting in a gathering of Ansar in Madina that Abu Musa (al-Ash'ari) arrived there and he was nervous. We asked him, what's the matter? He replied:

" 'Umar had called me, so I went to his house and greeted him three times but no one answered so I came back. 'Umar said: "Why didn't you come to see me?" I said: "I came and greeted three times at your door, but no one answered me so I came back, because the Messenger of Allah (SAAS) said: "If someone of you (tries) three times to seek the permission (to enter someone's house) and does not get the reply, then he should leave". 'Umar said: "Furnish the evidence or I will punish you". Ubayy b. Ka'ab said: "I said: "The youngest one (from the gathering) should accompany him". Abu Sa'id al-Khudri said: "I was the youngest one, so I went with him and told 'Umar that the Prophet (SAAS) has made that (statement)". *Ibid.* Bab al-Taslim wa'l-isti'dhan, Vol.11. pp 28-29.

24 *Mahr*: bridal money or other things given or promised to be given to wife by her husband on wedding.

25 *'Iddah*: a woman's period of waiting after divorce or death of her husband during which she is not allowed to remarry.

26 Literally the people of principles. The term is applied to the scholars of the Principles of Islamic Jurisprudence (*Usul al-Fiqh*).

27 *Al-Nafar:* an optional practice for pilgrims to stop and relax for a while at *al-abtah*- a mountain path and basin shaped valley, while returning to Makkah from Mina.

28 Walking at a quick pace, especially with the movement of arms and legs to demonstrate dignity and firmness.

29 *Mutamatti'* (from *tamattu'*) the one who performs *'umra* before *hajj* while wearing separate *ihram* for both.

30 *Qarin* (from *Qiran*) is the one who performs *hajj* along with *'umra* before it while wearing same *ihram* for both.

31 *Mufrid* (from *Ifrad*) the one who puts on *ihram* with the intention of performing *hajj* only and does not perform *'umra.*

32 *Ihlal*: loud utterance of *talbiyah* when one puts on *ihram* for *hajj.*

33 Literally to respond/ to comply with. It is taken from *'Labbayk'* which means 'O Lord! I am present/I am at your service'. It is the following invocation chanted by the pilgrims:

لبّيك اللهم لبّيك لا شريك لك لبّيك أن الحمد و النعمة لك والملك لا شريك لك

34 However, in several other *Ahadith*, the Prophet (SAAS) is reported to have urged his Companions to observe this practice for Muslims and non-Muslims alike. For example, it is reported on the authority of Jabir b.'Abd Allah (R.A) as saying: "Once a funeral procession was passing that the Messenger of Allah (SAAS) stood up for it. We said: "O Messenger of Allah, she was a Jewess. He said: "Death is frightening, when you see a funeral procession stand for it". Ghulam Rasul Sa'idi: *Sharh Sahih Muslim*. (Fareed Bookstall, Lahore, 1994-97) Vol.2.pp.769-772.

35 A valley in the country of Banu Hawazin between Makkah and Ta'if where the battle of Hunain took place in (Shawwal) 8th year of Hijra. *Sira* of Ibn Hisham, (ed. Mustafa al-Saqa and others, Mu'assasa 'Ulum al-Qur'an, Bayrut, no date.), Vol.2. p.487.

36 *Athar* plural of *athar* means traces or signs. It is applied to *Hadith* of the Prophet (SAAS) and the sayings of the Companions and Followers.

37 *Mufti*: a religious scholar who is competent in Islamic sciences in particular *Fiqh* to give *fatwa*.

37 *Musnad*: a *Hadith* which has uninterrupted *isnad* (chains of reporters) from the Prophet (SAAS).

39 *Mursal*: a *Hadith* in which the name of the Companion reporting *Hadith* directly from the Prophet (SAAS) is omitted.

40 *Mawquf*: a *Hadith* accredited back to a Companion.

41 *Muhaqala*: a forbidden sale in which the grain not fully-grown is sold against fully-grown grain.

42 *Muzabana*: a forbidden sale in which dry dates or other such things are sold by way of weight or measure for something of this kind whose weight or measure are not known.

43 A *Hadith* which is accredited back to the Prophet (SAAS) in its *isnad* and in which the Companion states that the Prophet (SAAS) said so and so.

44 This refers to the following *Hadith* narrated by Abu Huraira (R.A): The Messenger of Allah (SAAS) said: "If a dog drinks from a utensil of anyone of you it is essential to wash it seven times." Sa'idi, *op.cit.,* Bab Wulugh al-Kalb, Vol.1.p.957.

45 Literally partnership or tying of shoelaces together. Technically it means giving shares of inheritance to full brothers with their maternal brothers. Cf. Lisan al-'Arab of Ibn Manzur, and Sunan al-Darimi: Kitab al-Fara'id.

46 *Isnad* or *sanad*, means chains of reporters of *Hadith*.

47 *Al-Fuqaha' al-Sab'a* is referred to the following seven Jurists of Madina: (1) Sa'id b. Musayyab (2) 'Urwa b. Zubair b.al-'Awwam (3) Abu Bakr b. 'Abd al-Rahman b.al-Harith (4) Qasim b. Muhammad b. Abu Bakr al-Siddique (5) 'Ubaid Allah b. 'Abd Allah b. 'Utba b. Mas'ud al-Hudhali (6) Sulaiman b. Yasar, and (7) Kharija b. Zaid b. Thabit.

48 A jurist with absolute power of exposition.

49 *Munqati'*: a *Hadith* with an interrupted or discontinued chain of narrators.

50 *Khabar Wahid*: a tradition reported by a single person.

51 *Al-Baqara*: 180

52 In the text it reads فلم يعلموا بها

53 *Huffaz* plural of *hafiz*: the one who preserves or learns something by heart. A traditionist who remembers one hundred thousand reported *Ahadith* together with their *matn* and *sanad* and the conditions of *jarh* and *ta 'dil* (criticism and authentication), Sa'idi, *op.cit.* Vol.1 p.12

54 This refers to a *Hadith* narrated by Ibn 'Umar that the Prophet (SAAS) (in response to the question that whether the water in the desert consumed by cattle and other animals is pure or not) said: "When the (amount of) water is two *qulla* it does not get impure". Shah Abdul Haque *Muhaddith* Dihlawi: *Ashi'aat al-Lam'at Sharh Mishkat*: Urdu trans: Muhammad Sa'id Ahmad Naqshbandi and others, (Farid Bookstall, Lahore, 1981), Vol.1. p.975. *Qulla* is a vessel of earthenware or a bucket made of leather. It contains about 40-litre water.

55 *Hadith Khiyar al-Majlis*: choice of confirming or cancelling a deal in a business meeting. It is reported by Ibn 'Umar that the Prophet (SAAS) said: "When two persons get into a business deal, they (the seller and the buyer) have the choice (to cancel the deal) before they depart while they remain in the same place, or one of them says to the other: "Choose (i.e. whether you want to cancel or confirm the deal now)". If one of them gives the choice to the other and the other accepts it and confirms the deal, it will become binding. And if after the deal they get separated and none of them cancelled the deal then it will be binding". Sa' idi. *op.cit.,*, Vol. 4. P.170.

56 *Ra'i:* subjective opinion used in religious laws.

57 ل is missing. See *Hujjat Allah al-Baligha* of Shah Wali Allah, ed. Al-Sayyad al-Sabiq (Dar al-Kutub al-Haditha, Cairo, 1322 A.H.), part 2, p. 310

58 *Istihsan:* juristic inquiry, methods of reasoning, application of discretion in a legal decision as a result of personal deliberation, especially by the jurists of Hanafi *madhhab*.

59 *Gharib* from *gharaba*: something strange or rare. A *Hadith* reported from only one Companion or which is reported by a single transmitter at a later stage.

60 *Al- Mutaba'at wa'l-shawahid*. Traditionists are always in search for more witnesses in favour of a *Hadith*, which is reported by one source only. Such type of search is called '*I 'tibar'*. If they don't find any other witness for a particular *Hadith*, it is declared as *fard mutlaq* or *Gharib*. For example if a *Hadith* is reported by this *isnad-* Hammad b. Salama- Ayyub- Ibn Sirin- Abu Huraira-The Prophet, it would be looked for whether some other trustworthy person has reported from Ayyub or not. If someone is found, it will be called '*complete mutaba'a* '. If not found, it would be looked for whether someone other than Ayyub has reported it from Ibn Sirin or not. If it is found, it will be called '*incomplete mutaba'a* (*qasira*). In case the same words of *Hadith* or its meanings are reported by another Companion, it will be called '*shahid'*. Cf. Suhaib Hasan: *Criticism of Hadith among Muslims with reference to Sunan of Ibn Majah*, (Presidency of Islamic Research, IFTA and Propagation, Riyadh, Saudi Arabia, 1404/1984), p.156.Footnote 3 & 4.

61 Plural of fard: can be used of an *isnad* with only one transmitter at each stage, or of a tradition transmitted only by people of one district. J.Robson, op.cit., Vol.3.p.25.

62 *Ittisal: Isnad* going back to the Prophet (SAAS*)* without interruption, while *inqita'* means interruption in *isnad.*

63 *Marfu' Muttasil. Muttasil* is used for an unbroken *isnad* traced back to the source. If it goes back to the Prophet (SAAS) it is *muttasil marfu'*, if to a Companion it is *muttasil mawkuf"*. J.Robson. *op.cit.,* vol.3.p.25.,

64 In the text it reads Zaid b. Harun.

65 *Shadhah*: a *Hadith* which is reported by a trustworthy reporter but differs from what is reported by others.

66 *'Uluwwu sanad* or *isnad 'ali* (a high *isnad)*, which is used when there are very few links between the transmitter and the Prophet, or between him and a certain authority, is considered a valuable type on the ground that the fewer the links the fewer are possible chances of error. *Isnad nazil* (a lower *isnad*) means that there are many links. The quality of the former is called *'uluww* and of the later *nuzul*. J.Robson, *op .cit*.,Vol.3.p.26.

67 *Mustafida* from *istafada* (abundance, overflow) is usually applied to a *Hadith Sahih,* which has more than two narrators and it gets widespread currency and acceptability because of the reliability of narrators and authenticity of *isnad*. Some Traditionists treat it as equivalent to *mashhur*; others regard it as equivalent to *mutawatir*.

68 *Al-Layyin* (*al-Hadith*): (easy-going in tradition) is one of the four classes of lower authority, and deserves to have his traditions considered and compared with those of others. J.Robson, *op.cit.Vol.2.p.462.*

69 *Munkar*: a *Hadith* similar to *shadhah* except that the reporter who goes against other reporters in his report is not trustworthy, hence such report is to be rejected.

70 *Al-Mu'minun*: 53

71 To give preference. Technically it means making distinction or comparisons between two views or precedents.

72 *Al-Qiyas al-Iqtirani* and *al-Sharti* are the two terms of *Kalam* and *Mantiq*. A Syllogism (*al-Qiyas al-Mantiqi*) is called interpellative (hypothetical), if the conclusion itself or its contrary is actually mentioned in it, as "if this be a body, it is spacial". Here the very conclusion is mentioned in it. And if we say "but it is not spacial" it follows that it is not a body. In this instance the contradictory is mentioned in it. A Syllogogism is called conjugate (*Iqtirani*) if it is not like the preceding, *e.g.* "every body is composed of parts, every thing composed of parts is temporal," it follows "every body is temporal". Neither the conclusion nor its opposite is actually mentioned in it. Then according to propositions *Qiyas Iqtirani* is divided into *Hamli* and *Sharti*. If the premises of a syllogism are categorical, it is called categorical syllogism (*al-Qiyas al-Hamli*). *Qiyas Sharti* is composed of conditional and or categorical propositions. Cf. Muhammad 'Ali al-Thanwi, *Kashshaf Istilahat al-Funun*, ed. Mohammad Wajih and Gholam Kadir, Asiatic Society of Bengal, Calcutta, 1862, Vol.2.p.1192-3.

73 *Al-Musarrat* from *tasriya:* a sheep (or other animal) left unmilked for a long time. It is reported on the authority of Abu Huraira, (R.A), that the Messenger of Allah (SAAS) said: "Whoever buys an unmilked goat then he milks it, if he is satisfied with (the amount of) its milk he can keep it, otherwise he may return it with one *sa'* dates". Sa'idi: *Sharh Sahih Muslim.op.cit.* Vol.4.p.147. One *sa '* is equal to about 3 kilograms.

74 *Hadith Maqlub* (transposed) is applied when a tradition is attributed to someone other than the real authority to make it an acceptable *gharib* tradition, or when two traditions have the *isnad* of the one with the *matn* of the other. J.Robson, *op.cit.*Vol.3, p.26

75 I.e.*Ashab al-Tarjih*: those who are competent to make comparisons and distinguish the correct (*sahih*) and the preferred (*rajih, arjah*) and the agreed upon (*mufta biha*) views from the weak ones. Mohammad Hashim Kamali, *Principles of Islamic Jurisprudence* (Islamic Texts Society, Cambridge, 1991, Revised edition), p.389.

76 *Ikhtiar:* Selection, choice or preference. This refers to the process of selecting, choosing and adoption of a juristic ruling or a precedent by a *faqih* in accordance with the principles of his *madhhab.*

77 In the text it reads قد يكون واجبا و قد يكون واجبا

78 A poem in which the second line of each distich rhymes with the same letter.

79 A stanza of four lines.
80 In the text it reads وارأى
81 *Mafhum al-Shart* (implication of the Condition). When the ruling of a text is contingent on a condition, then the ruling obtains only in the presence of that condition, and lapses otherwise. An example of this is the Qur'anic text on the entitlement to maintenance of divorced women who are observing their waiting period (*'iddah*). The text proclaims: 'If they are pregnant, then provide them with maintenance until they deliver the child' (*Al-Talaq*, 65:6). The condition here is pregnancy and the *hukm* applies only when this condition is present. Kamali, op.cit. p.136.
82 *Mafhum al-wasf* or *Mafhum al-Sifah* (Implication of the Attribute). When the ruling of a text is dependent on the fulfilment of a quality or an attribute then the ruling in question obtains only when that quality is present; otherwise it lapses. This can be shown in the Qur'anic text on the prohibited degrees of relations in marriage, which includes 'the wives of your sons proceeding from your lions' (*Al-Nisa'* 2:23). The pronounced meaning of this text is the prohibition of the wife of one's own son in marriage. The son has thus been qualified in the text by the phrase 'proceeding from your lions'. *Ibid*. p.136
83 *Hajj*: 77, in the text the verse has been wrongly quoted as اسجدوا واركعوا
84 While the significance of stillness in *ruku'* and *sajda* is emphasised by *Fuqaha'*, they do not treat the *Hadith* as explanation or description of *ruku'*. Rather the *Hadith* in their view means that the prayer of a person is not complete if he does not observe stillness in *ruku'* and *sajda*. They say the minimum requirement for *ruku'* and *sajda* to be valid is that one stays in these postures equal to the amount of time spent in reciting *Subhan Allah* at least once. The *ruku'* will be valid if one stretches his hands they reach his knees. In *sajda* both hands, nose and forehead are to be placed properly, while the toes of feet are positioned towards the *Ka'ba*.
85 *Al-Ma'ida*: 6 The full sentence in the above verse reads as follows: "As to the thief, man or woman, cut off their hands as a punishment for what they have done." Here again the *Fuqaha'* treat the *Ahadith* as explanation to the Qur'anic command as to the minimum amount of theft for which this punishment will be given to the thief. For example, Imam Muslim reported 'A'isha (R.A) that the Messenger of Allah (SAAS) cut off the hand of a thief for quarter of *dinar* and upwards.
86 Here they argue that the Qur'anic verse is general and the *Hadith* is its explanation. According to Imam Shafi'i mere rubbing of head is obligatory even if it is done on a single hair. According to Imam Abu Hanifa, rubbing of ? of head is obligatory. Imam Malik, Ahmad b. Hanbal and others regard rubbing of complete head necessary. Those who do not regard rubbing of complete head necessary argue on the basis of *Ahadith* narrated by Mughira b. Shu'ba which confirm that the Prophet (SAAS) rubbed only his forelock during *wudu*.
87 *Al-Nur*: 2 the full sentence in the above verse reads as follows: "The woman and the man guilty of *zina* (fornication or adultery) flog each of them with a hundred stripes". Since *zina* includes both fornication and adultery, therefore the *Fuqaha'* here use the *Ahadith* as well as the practice of the Prophet (SAAS) as explanation to the Qur'anic verse, which they say is general. Accordingly, if one or both of the parties involved in *zina*, are married, it will be adultery, the punishment for which is stoning to death, in the light of the saying and practice of the Prophet (SAAS). And if one or both of them are not married, it will be fornication, for which each one of them will be flogged with 100 lashes.
88 *Al-Ma'ida*: 41
89 *Al-Baqara*: 230. This refers to the following verse: " So if a husband divorces his wife (irrevocably), after that it is not permissible for him to remarry her until after she has

married another husband and he has divorced her." Because there is concordance between *Ahadith* and this verse, the *Fuqaha'*, therefore, treat them as explanation of Qur'an.

90 *Al-Muzzammil*: 20

91 Here the *Fuqaha'*, especially Ahanaf, reconcile between the Qur'anic verse and the above *Hadith*. They maintain that the command to recite Qur'an in prayer is general and unspecific. If recitation of *al-Fatiha* is made obligatory, it will mean abrogation of Qur'anic verse or addition to it by *Khabar Wahid*. In addition, in support of their view they refer to a *Hadith* narrated by Abu Huraira (R.A). Accordingly, a man after saying his prayer greeted the Prophet (SAAS). The Prophet (SAAS) returned his greeting and told him to go back and pray again because he has not offered the prayer (properly). After repeating this action three times, the man said: "By Him Who has sent you with Truth, whatever better I can do than this, please teach me". In response the Prophet (SAAS) taught him how to pray including recitation of Qur'an, but the *Hadith* did not mention by the Prophet (SAAS) recitation of *al-Fatiha*. See Bukhari and Muslim: Kitab al-Salah

92 Plural of *wasq* which is equal to sixty *sa's* and one *sa'* is equal to about 3 kilograms.

93 According to Imam Malik, Shafi'i and Ahmad b. Hanbal, minimum *nisab* (rate) for *'ushr* in agricultural yield is five *awsaq*. In view of Imam Abu Hanifa, there is no *nisab* in agricultural yield. Whatever is produced from land, *'ushr* or ? of it will be levied on it. His argument is based on the interpretation of the following Qur'anic verse: "O You who believe! Give of the pure things which you have earned, and of the fruits of the earth which We have produced for you". Al-Baqara: 267. He maintained that the word *ma* (meaning whatever) in this verse is general and hence to restrict the yield to five *awsaq* would imply addition to Qur'an on the basis of *Khabar Wahid*.

94 *Al-Baqara*: 196. This refers to a situation when the pilgrim is prevented from completing the *hajj* for some reason such as what happened to Muslims during the truce of Hudaibiya. 'Ali b. Abi Talib (R.A.) is reported to have said that (offering of sacrifice here means) goat, and in view of the opinion of Imam Abu Hanifa, Shafi'i, Malik and Ahmad b. Hanbal, it also includes other animals such as cow and camel. This view seems to be based on a *Hadith* reported by Sa'id b. Jubair (R.A.). Accordingly, the Prophet (SAAS) ordered the Companions during the truce of Hudaibiya to share a cow among seven of them.

95 *Al-Nisa'*: 25. Here is the complete sentence of this verse. "If anyone of you does not have the means to marry free believing women, they may marry believing women from among those whom your right hand possess". This means women captured as prisoners of war in *Jihad* under the orders of a Muslim Caliph.

96 *Al-'Ashr fi'l-'ashr*: ten by ten. This refers to the famous *Fiqhi* formula that the water of a pool, measuring 10 yards width and 10 yards length, is pure.

97 *Takbirat al-Tashriq* is the following invocation chanted after each prayer from the *Fajr* prayer of 9th Dhul-Hijja until the *'Asr* prayer of 13th Dhul-Hijja:

الله اكبر الله اكبر لا اله الا الله والله اكبر الله اكبر و لله الحمد

98 *Nikah al-Mahram*: those for whom marriage with a woman is forbidden because of kinship relationship such as father, son, brother and others who come in the same category.

99 *Tashshaud* of Ibn 'Abbas is slightly different from that of Ibn Mas'ud.

100 *'Ta'min'* to utter *'amin'* loudly after the imam completes reciting *'al-Fatiha'* in congregational prayer.

101 *Qunut*: a special *du'a* (supplication) offered in *'Isha* or *Fajr* prayer.

102 *Al-Zukhruf*: 23